MW01265566

LOVED
NOT
LOST

THE LIES WE BELIEVE THAT SHAPE THE
LIVES THAT WE LEAD

A TESTIMONY

Julia Kawamura

ISBN 979-8-89309-791-7 (Paperback)
ISBN 979-8-89309-792-4 (Digital)

Copyright © 2024 Julia Kawamura
All rights reserved
First Edition

All rights reserved. No part of this publication may be reproduced, distributed, or transmitted in any form or by any means, including photocopying, recording, or other electronic or mechanical methods without the prior written permission of the publisher. For permission requests, solicit the publisher via the address below.

Covenant Books
11661 Hwy 707
Murrells Inlet, SC 29576
www.covenantbooks.com

To Jenny and Josh and all those we've lost along the way before they knew how very much He loves them...although they do now.

CHAPTER 1

How Did I Get Here?

December 2012

Wow, what a year it had been. As I sat on the beach with my journal, pen in one hand, and my coffee cup in the other, I was peaceful and at ease. I felt warm and happy for the first time in months. So odd, this was my first morning on Kaua'i, and it seemed like home. The coffee cup had something positive and inspirational written on it. I had collected them that year and started each morning with a different one in hopes of finding solace, hope, and relief from the pain. I was watching the sunrise, feeling the warm breeze on my face and the sand on my bare feet. My mind could not wrap around the moment. I thought of all the shameful, sinful things I've done this year; how do I deserve this?

The year started off in deceit and dishonesty. I had left my first husband, the man I had been with for twenty-two years. Of course, I said it was because of this and that. I claimed I was just not happy, but actually, I had left because I had been involved with another man. You see, I jumped blindly into the arms of the first man who spoke flattery and gave me the attention that I craved and did so without any logic or conscience. I justified my actions by saying, "I deserve this. I work so hard, and no one has ever loved or appreciated me like this…" But within a few weeks, I knew I had made a big mistake.

By February of that year, my sin felt too great to carry. I called the man I was married to and told him everything. Although he said he forgave me, the pain of what I had done was too much to move on from for him. The weight of my sin combined with the vacillation of his forgiveness was crushing.

In hopes of some sort of redemption, I went to the only source I knew for forgiveness. I called an elder of the congregation I belonged to and confessed the truth behind the end of the marriage. Next in the process of forgiveness from God, according to the religion I was a part of, was to meet with a body of elders (comprised of three men), tell them all my sin, and communicate my sorrow in such a way that I would be deemed repentant. If they saw me as repentant, I could be allowed to stay in the congregation. If I was unrepentant, I would be disfellowshipped or excommunicated from the congregation. The judgment they handed down would be, according to them, from God.

The night I met with the elders and was told I would be allowed to stay in the congregation was also the night I discovered that my estranged husband decided to embark on an extramarital affair of his own. He felt that to be able to forgive me, he needed to do this to even the playing field. He was so broken by my infidelity that he believed this would make us even and help him forgive me. What a bittersweet night that was. I was, of course, devastated; but at the same time, I knew it was my life-altering decision that took the marriage to this point. So I believed I deserved it.

I spent that weekend torn and unsure of everything I thought was reality. I couldn't take back what I had done, the hurt to so many that I had caused. But I also had gotten a taste of living outside of all the rules and laws I had been under for forty years. There was a sense of freedom, and I liked it. Yet I couldn't escape the emptiness in my heart. The backlash from my religion and the view I had of who I was, who I thought God wanted me to be, and who God is was ever present and haunted me.

For the next two months, I wandered around in a state of broken and breaking. My soon-to-be ex-husband and I were constantly jabbing at each other emotionally, and with each jab, I would reach out to the other man for validation and acceptance—only to realize the void was too big, and he wasn't able to fill it either. I would then walk away from him as well, blaming him for my emptiness. It was a vicious cycle.

My parents knew I was in crisis, and although my dad is an elder and in charge of shepherding the flock, they both stayed away from me. Shepherding his congregation of people who adored him was so much easier than loving the child that was bitter and angry and acting out.

Most of our friends had taken sides, his or mine. But honestly, it was easier to side with the victim of adultery—him.

I was lost and felt like I had no map or compass without the religion and those within it telling me what to do. Everything that always was clearly black or white was now gray and blurry.

So in May, I decided to own my truth to the best of my ability. I wasn't sure what my future was, but I knew I wanted the attention of the other man. I rationalized that at least I was being honest about who I was and what I was doing. I was so angry at all the double standards, half-truths, and hypocrisy around me for decades by friends, family, and religion. Breaking free from my marriage, as well as this organization, was the way I decided I would find myself. I even had a tattoo of a large bright-red letter *J* tattooed onto my chest, wearing my "scarlet letter" with pride that I had sinned but owned it and was living honestly, or so I believed. But the tattoo didn't give me the empowerment I longed for. Nothing I did in those days made me feel whole again. The pain and emptiness were a gaping hole that couldn't be filled.

I went to the body of elders a second time and told them I was still seeing the other man and not going to stop. This time, I was obviously unrepentant and, therefore, would be disfellowshipped—removed from the congregation.

There was a one-week window between the decision they made and when the announcement would be read to the congregation. I used this time to send texts of goodbye to several of my lifelong friends, many of which refused to come and meet with me. Most responded that the situation was too sad; they didn't want to see me. My mom was one of the ones that opted not to come to me. My dad came to my workplace to see me the last day before it was announced. I stood in front of him thirty pounds lighter than the last time he had laid eyes on me six months before. I was broken and emotionally unsteady. I will never forget his words as I cried into his shoulder: "I sure hope you repent and come back to Jehovah before Armageddon comes and kills you." The words pierced through the air like knives and landed one by one into my heart. So much rejection from a man that I thought loved me, another reason to believe God had abandoned me too.

I sat with the other man in his truck outside of the church, listening to the church meeting on his car radio the night it was read to the congregation "Julia Brashear is no longer" one of them. I looked at the other man with instant regret. The realization of having left everything I knew as truth sank in. I didn't know the truth from lies anymore. I wanted to run, but where? From that moment on, I would basically not exist in the eyes of my family and lifelong friends. God would no longer see me, hear me, or answer me. Darkness descended like a heavy black cloak.

Within a month, a close friend of mine suggested what I needed was a break from routine, a hard reset. She suggested I take a vacation and leave town, put my phone down for a week or more, and let myself heal. I have always been very close to my twin nieces on the East Coast. They graduated from the eighth grade that year, so I hopped on a plane to New Hampshire for the event. They are not the same religion as my parents and, therefore, have no limitations on being with me, making this the perfect getaway. Nonetheless, I arrived full of shame and uncertainty. But the girls were so loving and innocent. We laughed and snuggled all week. No judgment of my sins, no second-guessing who I was to them based on the mistakes of the last six months. In pictures, you can see me transition from deep anguish at the beginning of the visit to the lights coming back on behind my eyes five days later. In hindsight, that trip saved me from the spiraling downward of self-destruction that I was in.

Although truthfully, the pivotal moment came from their grandmother, Irene. The night of the graduation party, she came into the kitchen and caught me alone. She said, "I know why you two are getting divorced." I immediately went into defense-and-deflect mode. She stopped me and said, "You made a mistake. Everyone sins. But God forgives and loves you anyway, so get over it and move on." I was shocked and touched all at once. Although her words were blunt and hard to hear, I felt loved and grounded. Forgiven and loved, that was not the God I was raised to believe in. That was especially true now. Her words opened my mind and heart to the possibility of a God of love, mercy, and grace. I was not sure I was deserving of this kind of God. Was He even real?

I spent the next few months going back and forth from the man that I had the affair with to my ex-husband and then to the congregation meetings, trying to fit in with them again. I would leave each meeting (and one convention) crying and feeling there's no way I fit there anymore, that there must be something wrong with me. Was I, like my mom's friend suggested years before, amoral?

I jumped from bar to bar, from bed to bed, trying to feel something. I took up running long distances and ran a half marathon on the day my divorce was final, mentally and emotionally purging all the damage that I had done that led up to the end of my marriage. With every passing mile, I would pull something ugly out of my soul, reflect on it, and discard it alongside the road as I ran, trying to find the truth about me. About life. About God.

In August, the company I had worked for most of my adult life approached me with an offer I couldn't refuse, the manager-in-waiting or MIW program. Once enrolled, I would be placed as a store manager somewhere unknown within three to six months. The idea of living anywhere else but my hometown sent a jolt of excitement and optimism through me. I just wanted to get out of Humboldt County where every aisle I shopped in the grocery store and every block I walked down on the street, I was confronted by one of my lifelong friends that reacted as if I didn't exist anymore. They either looked right through me or, worse yet, like I was something contagious. Some even visibly moving away from me so as not to be contaminated by my sin. I jumped at the opportunity to get out of town.

The day before Thanksgiving, I got the phone call I had been waiting for: How did I feel about Kaua'i? Would I be open to that move? I was ecstatic! I have always craved sunlight and love the beach. I had won several incentive trips working for this company, taking me someplace warm and tropical and never wanted to come home. I never had allowed myself to dream of living every day in paradise.

How could this be, though? How was I not going to be sent to some big city or a desolate town as the outcast I believed I was? But instead, I was being whisked away, rescued even, and taken to a beautiful island where I would get paid well and find myself, maybe even healed?

I called each of the men I had been bouncing back and forth from, met up with them, apologized for the last year, and ended the relationship with each of them.

As I drove my new, shiny, white Camaro to the port that would ship it to my new home, I felt a glimmer of optimism. Although I was going to be truly alone for the first time in my life (no family, friends, or male companions), I wasn't afraid or depressed anymore.

So now here I was, sitting on a beach on Kaua'i not even two weeks after that phone call. The company had taken care of every aspect of the move, unprecedented before that or since then. I sat there asking God, "Are you there?" and "Have you really left me?" I thought about the last year, the pain I had caused and the pain I was in. I wondered now if there was a God that loved me like Irene had said, and if so, was He pursuing me? In that moment, I prayed for the first time in months. I told God in this beautiful place I now called home that I would look for Him. I would give him a chance to reveal who He really is. In that very instant, a whale came out of the water and breached right out in front of me! I looked around at all the other people watching the sun rise to see if they had just seen it too or had I imagined it. *Was that you, God?*

You see, I was taught that if I was disfellowshipped, God wouldn't even look at me, let alone listen to my prayer or reveal His love for me. Asking God for signs and Him honoring those requests? Not acceptable.

What was I to think now?

This is the moment that would change everything I ever knew or believed. Somehow, in that simple act, I knew I was loved, not abandoned nor lost. My heart and mind began to open to receiving the truth about God.

That was the beginning of my journey with my Lord, Savior, and Father.

But to understand how I came to this point of my life, we have to go back to the beginning.

CHAPTER 2

The Orange Starfish

The beginning of my story started years before my conception.

I know what you are thinking: "How could she possibly have a testimony before she was even born?" Well, what I'm about to tell you has been told to me by my parents many times, almost like a bedtime story.

My mom was a single mother with two young girls under the age of three. My dad was a single father with a daughter as well. They knew each other vaguely from high school but were indifferent to each other. They were reintroduced in November of 1969 at a circuit assembly (regional, multi-congregation gathering) and decided within six weeks to get married before the end of the year. They married on December 31, 1969. This was not a whirlwind romance by any means. There wasn't a lot of emotion involved. They would later talk to my sisters and I about the practicality of marriage without a hint of spark or romance being the ideal. They weren't catapulted by love or even lust but by the drive to have a mate in the same religion and to remain clean (no sex before marriage). It was so unemotional that they even used the wedding bands from one of their previous marriages for their ceremony. Their honeymoon consisted of a fishing trip in which my dad thought it would be great for my mom to watch him as he fished. When they arrived, my mom had forgotten to pack any casual shoes, and they had to go to the drugstore for some inexpensive sneakers. My dad was instantly irritated at the extra expenditure, and my mom wasn't thrilled to watch her new husband fish for hours in the freezing January weather.

They both came into the marriage with unrealistic ideals for each other. My mom was newly baptized and had heard all about how a man that loves Jehovah would be an ideal "Christian head," a provider and leader to her and her girls. My dad had been taught that a "Christian wife" would take care of *all* his needs and give him all the support, respect and love that he longed for.

Although later in life Mom would often say that they "grew to love and appreciate each other," they were both disappointed from the beginning.

They came home to the reality of a blended family with its many challenges. Neither of them had any skills to help them navigate the complexities of a marriage with so much turmoil, nor would they be provided with any through their friends or religious organization. They had no tools, no support, no couple's groups. They had only the three meetings a week they needed to be at with their new family dressed and well behaved where they would be indoctrinated with illusions of a possibility of everlasting life in a paradise earth if they just followed *all the rules*. My dad was one of the leaders in the congregation. Between working full time and his responsibilities in the congregation, child-rearing fell on my mom.

At the annual convention (gathering of a larger group of congregations), summer of 1970, Mom discovered she was pregnant with me. We would soon become a family of his, hers, and ours. There was never any excitement or happiness expressed around this event by anyone who told the story, only burden and stress. This was not a happy discovery as they were already a family of five and struggling in every way.

In March 1971, I was born. My mom talks about how I did a full somersault one day into labor, changed my mind for a few days, coming two days later. My dad will proudly tell you he was one of the first men of his generation allowed in the delivery room. He will tell you how cool childbirth was and the state it left my mom's body in. Also, as the story went on, the umbilical cord was wrapped around my neck, and the doctor had to work quickly to help me breathe. None of the stories are of joy or awe at the first sight of the child they created together. Neither of them will speak about the relief of my first cries. Their faith tells them that if their children do not follow the teachings of their organization, they will have to let their children go… so this is the way our relationship started. It is the nature of their faith—don't get too attached.

So the earliest memories I have of my dad are of him playing with me and calling me his nickname for me, his dudems, in between commercials while watching the news, taking us to the meetings and to his favorite places to camp and fish, but never ever did I feel he was emotionally attached to us or that we were unconditionally loved. Love was something we earned through obedience to the religious organization. Love was a feeling of doing something for your parents and others, such as making them laugh or taking care of them, not embarrassing or shaming them with childlike shenanigans or by your flawed personality. As a matter of fact, there are three or four pictures in existence of any of their small children, but there are hundreds of pictures taken by my dad with one of his expensive cameras of all his favorite mountains/rivers, creation.

In hindsight, maybe he was always struggling with finding God's love for himself. Maybe all the pictures of creation were his way of seeking God.

Now there were four children that my mom had to primarily care for and get ready for all the meetings. We had to go in dresses or skirts and my dad in a suit. My siblings and I sat in front of our parents so they could ensure we were quiet and still for the one- to three-hour meeting of the evening. All meetings were prepared for an audience of adults; no variations were made for children. If we whispered or acted like children in any way, we were promptly reminded of where we were by mom's pencil popping us on our ear. In addition, we all had to study for every one of those meetings, which left little to no time to play as little kids should.

My mom was exhausted, stressed, and disappointed most of my childhood.

When I was about four, my dad was going fishing, and I jumped at the possibility of going with him. I never knew when I would get playtime with Dad, but I knew if we were doing something he enjoyed, the chances were good. My mom expressed misgivings about him taking me because he was going to the Samoa jetty, which was known to be treacherous to even the most alert adults. But my pleads to go won out, and Dad loaded me up in the car. Typical of my dad, he told me, "Don't go near the rocks" and sent me off on my own as he searched out the best fishing spot.

So of course, I quickly found my way up next to the rocks. Once up there, I saw the most beautiful orange starfish twinkling in the water and instantly had to have it. But as I bent down to pick it up, a wave came out of nowhere and swept me into the bay. I panicked; I knew I was in trouble. I tried to grab at anything to pull myself up, but the blades of grass I could grab would quickly break off in my tiny hands, and the sea would pull me in backward. This vivid memory would replay in my nightmares for years. A stranger appeared, rescued me from the waves, and asked me where my parents were. I remember him coming from the water. Dad says he doesn't know and honestly doesn't remember him at all. I pointed out my dad standing several yards down the jetty, happily fishing. As the stranger walked me to my dad, my dad looked over and saw me soaking wet. There was shock and fear on his face.

The next thing I remember is feeling my dad's irritation. I assumed it was from his fishing trip being cut short because of my disobedience. The drive home was a combination of silence and chastisement. The moment we arrived home, and my mom saw me, she grabbed me and threw me in a tub with hot water. I was too young to know she had a legitimate fear of hypothermia and possibly even intense regret that she had not stood her ground when she felt she shouldn't let me go. I just thought I had been bad, broke the rules, and now I was in a scalding tub of water; and my parents were fighting again. I heard them yelling at each other in the next room. They had no tools to handle crisis or to know how to communicate with each other. During my entire childhood, yelling and fighting were a constant presence in moments of fear or heartbreak.

For years after this, I felt like every time there was conflict, I was either responsible for it, or I needed to fix it.

When I was going through counseling in 2011, the jetty memory was so graphically recalled from my subconscious that I was having nightmares on a regular basis. I emailed my parents and told them that my whole life, I had felt abandoned and as if I needed to take care of myself, and I believed it stemmed from that fateful day. My mom confirmed my suspicion that she had not wanted Dad to take me; she had a bad feeling.

My dad responded, "I'm sorry after all these years that this incident is still bothering you. I'm not trying to make you feel bad, but I did tell you not to go near the waves, and you disobeyed. I do recall you got a little wet, but I thought you were just scared." For the first time, I was angry at my dad. How could he blame a child? He expected me to take care of myself at four. He took zero responsibility for my care, or lack thereof, and that realization was painful. Maybe he didn't want to dig up past mistakes. Maybe it was too much for him. His response felt like abandonment all over again, and I emailed back that I needed some time to process without any more dialogue with them.

Years later (July 2021), my niece got married; and my now husband Keith, our daughter, and I came to the wedding. Due to some unavoidable issues, the reception had to be moved to the Samoa beach. As we approached the area, I felt uneasy, almost ill. I said a prayer and carried on. During the reception, I walked over to the water and looked down. There was a bright orange starfish sparkling in the water. A chill ran down my spine as I realized that this was "the jetty." Driving home after, discussing the experience with my little family, we entertained many reasons that God may have brought this beautiful occasion to that beach. I believe the Lord wanted me to know, unquestionably, that He has always been there for me and always will be. That is who He really is.

The lie I had believed was that every time someone was upset or angry, I must've done something to provoke it, or in some way or another, I deserved their outburst. I've taken responsibility for others' bad behavior from childhood. Even now, I struggle to not take it personally when others are rude because they are just having a bad day. The echoes of the adults in my childhood have laid the groundwork for me to believe I am responsible for others' feelings.

The truth is that children are a gift from God, *always*. Being a loving parent is difficult. Mistakes will be made. But caring for a child is something you get entrusted with, and the Lord takes that trust seriously. Sure, there will be a lot of highs and lows as well as unpredictable and unavoidable drama involved in parenting, even the most well-be-haved children. But none of the fear, anxiety, or reaction to the trials of child rearing are a child's "fault."

> "Children are a gift from the Lord; they are a reward from him. Children born to a young man are like arrows in a war-rior's hands. How joyful is the man whose quiver is full of them" (Psalm 127:3–5 NLT).

At the end of the day, I thank God for saving me then, now, and always. When I feel stressed and fearful now, I try to reflect on the fact that God will guide me and protect me until my last breath. He knows me, and He *loves* me. I am a gift from Him.

CHAPTER 3

Fighting Frisky

Frisky, adjective
playful and full of energy:
"he bounds about like a frisky pup"

synonyms:
lively bouncy bubbly perky active energetic animated zestful full of vim and vigor playful full of fun coltish skittish spirited high-spirited in high spirits exuberant frolicsome gamesome sportive frolic wanton

(Oxford Languages Dictionary)

I love laughter. I love to laugh hard into my belly. I love to make people laugh. I love to listen to other people laughing. Laughter brings me so much joy.

But it hasn't always been an asset to me…

Some of my best memories from childhood involve joking around, impersonating other people in the room, and making people laugh. My mom's friends would warn her that I was frisky, and she needed to keep an eye on me; that trait was going to get me in trouble and shame the family and God's name. That's usually when the fun stopped, and "settle down now" or some form of that would be enforced.

But those fleeting moments of laughter were welcomed in the dark times we lived and grew up in.

It was the late seventies. The world was recovering from war, and people were trying to find their happy place. There was so much bad news on the TV and newspapers. My favorite time as a frisky little girl was sitting on my dad's lap watching the news. You see, during the commercials, it was playtime. For those two minutes, I had his attention to make him laugh, be tickled by him, and just be a kid. But as soon as the news came back on, it was time to "settle down" (first warning); "I said be quiet now the news is back on" (second warning); "Okay, go to your room" (if I didn't pipe down). I couldn't help it, really; the news was so sad I didn't want to watch it. I wanted to laugh and make him laugh.

But that wasn't the only time my personality wasn't acceptable; the religious meetings were also no time for silliness.

We had five meetings a week that we attended. The entire family would rush to the meetings after a day of work or school, after eating dinner and getting dressed for the event. There would be high anxiety in the car on the way there because Mom was a nervous wreck from her household responsibilities, which included getting four girls fed, changed, and in the car. My dad always needed to arrive early for the meetings. Dad usually worked that day then came home to bathe and go over whatever part he had in the meeting that evening (or elder's meeting he would have after). The meetings were always serious business. We needed to sit paying attention like all the adults.

The meetings were as follows:

- Sunday would begin with a stoic song, an hour talk, another song, the study of the week, and another song.
- Tuesday would be the book study, which was an hour-long question-and-answer of the book of the moment, one chapter a week.
- Thursday would be the ministry school with assignments to students that would never graduate (seriously, it is infinite, no end), a song, and the service meeting, a collection of assignments given to only those in good standing in the congregation.
- In addition to these meetings, preparation of the material for those meetings was expected so one could have a full share of the meetings. Everyone that wanted to show their worth as a member of the congregation was expected to participate. Young and old, extroverts or introverts, no excuses— if you were a good Christian, you participated. Friday night, there was preparation for going door-to-door, and Saturday, we went door-to-door, no exceptions. No sleeping in, no cartoons. We had

lives to save with the literature we shared with unsuspecting homeowners that answered their doors.

- We also had family study on Monday nights, which was another evening of quiet organized question-and-answer from Dad's book of choice. Those lasted about an hour every week.

I am an extrovert, so I loved participating in the meetings. I did have a very difficult time not whispering or giggling during them, but a few pops to the head from Mom's pencil, and I quickly learned to pay attention. My older sisters were not as outgoing. Their personality, coupled with the scars from being abandoned by their biological fathers, made the meetings and the expectations at those meetings even more uncomfortable for my sisters. Many of the drives home would include a firm scolding and sometimes even loss of privileges because of their lack of participation at the meeting. My dad would then hold me up as a shining example of participation, and I would glow from his adoration.

To say this made for some intense sibling rivalry is putting it mildly. I had both of my natural parents still together. I enjoyed being in the limelight; hence, my participation was always exuberant. And I was frisky all the time, which drew attention to me. My mere existence was a bone of contention to my sisters. My mom was an introvert; so she, too, was exhausted by my energy.

I learned young that being frisky wasn't welcome around God's house or in His presence. I had to fight my urge to be silly constantly. I believed early on that I needed to hide who I truly was to be accepted by Him, the congregation, and my family.

Growing up, we had three fir trees in our backyard that had grown tall (I think twenty feet) and intertwined with each other. We couldn't really afford toys in our home, so those trees were my playhouse. They were a place for me to climb up and hide, fantasizing about performing, dancing, and laughing. There in those trees, I was free to be silly, and no one would see or judge me. It was here, hidden in the fir needles, that I would ask God if He created all things why He would create me to be so bad, it didn't seem fair. I longed to be silly and then felt so guilty when I was. As a child, I didn't feel like I fit in anywhere. I wanted to play like all the other neighbor kids and have birthdays and holidays and parties. But if I even uttered a word of this to my parents, the disapproval and disappointment was loud and clear. There would be a full discussion about how wrong those things were.

The story of Herod's birthday was told, and the loss of John's head at it was the consequence of all birthdays in God's eyes. They would read the Bible passages in which they told me God said, "Don't be misled, bad association spoils useful habits" (1 Corinthians 15:33, their translation). Occasionally, though not often, I could sneak one of the neighbor kids into my evergreen hideaway, and we would imagine each of the trees were our own little houses. We would play for hours in those trees, laughing so hard as we reenacted the movie or sitcom of the month, or some other make-believe scenario. It was, however, rare to have these playdates because the neighbors were not of the same religion as us, and therefore, they were "bad association." Too much time spent with anyone not of our religion would "spoil" the good habits they worked so hard to instill in us with all the weekly meetings.

One day, as I walked home from school, I came around the bend toward my house to see the complete devastation of fairy-tale time: Someone had cut down the trees while I was at school. I came running down the hill toward home, tears streaming down my face. My mom, perplexed, asked me what was wrong.

I said, "Someone cut down the trees!"

I will never forget her face, so annoyed at my dramatic antics. "Of course, we did! They were blocking the sun and gave us nothing but mildew and darkness!" To her, the trees were a nuisance. My mom was completely unaware of what they brought to her child who had no other outlet to express herself.

That was the end of my private space, my freedom. I learned from that day on how to turn my silliness on and off. To be frisky and funny when everyone was sad and needed a laugh, but to be silent during the important meetings and matters of God.

The lie I was believing is that there was something wrong with me. I was defective from birth, unable to truly please God because I was so impulsive and mischievous. For years, when I would indulge in loud outbursts of laughter, I felt shame when met with frowns, raised eyebrows, and criticisms, always feeling the need to apologize for my friskiness.

The truth is, we are who God created us to be. Our loving heavenly Father created us exactly the way we are supposed to be to do everything He purposed us to. If we are frisky? He made that part of us too. True, we don't need to indulge our every whim, or whim of our child, but we shouldn't stifle them in some false sense of worship to God. He is a happy God after all.

> "Bring all who claim me as their God, for I have made them for my glory. It was I who created them". (Isaiah 43:7 NLT)

> "For we are God's handiwork, created in Christ Jesus to do good works, which God prepared in advance for us to do." (Ephesians 2:10 NIV)

We can't get so caught up in all the meetings, participation, or self-imposed/interpreted rules of God that we forget to just be His and how He created us.

CHAPTER 4

Only Snitches Get Spiritual Stitches

I was elementary school age when deflecting and finger-pointing became a part of survival in life. Of course, all kids try to get away with what they can, pushing boundaries to know their limits. But I was in a home full of very strict rules that governed our every living moment, reinforced by an organization ready to judge and punish any mistake, intentional or not. Living by these rules and laws was considered basic, and deviating was not tolerated in any way. Every rule was nonnegotiable. This was also an unattainable standard in which judgment loomed heavily around every decision.

"Seek Jehovah, all you meek ones of the earth, who have practiced His own judicial decision. Seek righteousness, seek meekness. *Probably* you may be concealed in the day of Jehovah's anger" (Zephaniah 2:3, their translation, emphasis added).

This scripture was used regularly throughout the literature we were indoctrinated with at meetings. Think about the way that is written and how that would affect the minds and hearts of young and old alike. The message was clear: Do everything this organization tells you to (because we are God's mouthpiece), and "probably" you will be accepted by God, but there is no promise. Judgment awaited any independent thought, motive, and action taken. This way of life created an environment from the congregation to the family circle of tattle-telling, finger-pointing, and snitching if you will. How could there not be? Human nature often creates in us a little bit of a deflector when we are confronted with opposition or accountability. None of us could live up to the demands of those teachings, so we all looked for the defect in each other to feel a little bit superior in our own state of imperfection.

As a child, I would hear my dad talking to other adults on occasion about Jehovah's spirit being withdrawn from the congregation, and a hunt for the culprit would ensue. At ten, I vividly remember my mind's image of an angry God: to be feared by all. I imagined some of the powerful kings from history books that hunted down and punished any in the land that dared defy him. It was in these dark days of God's supposed withdrawal from the congregation that the finger-pointing and backstabbing would begin out of some perverse loyalty to God.

On one occasion, I sat outside of a bar with my oldest sister on a makeshift stakeout, waiting for one of her good friends to exit the establishment because she just knew he was in there drinking and dancing. Bars were bad, and she needed evidence of his loose conduct so she could take him to the elders. Once she saw him and turned him in, they would deal with him and his behavior, which would theoretically restore God's spirit back into the congregation.

Those who went to the elders and told anything they knew, whether they saw the sin or heard of the sin, were told how good of a Christian they were and considered to be an example of loyalty to Jehovah and the congregation. And if you didn't? Well, that was a different outcome...

One of my sisters was disfellowshipped twice, not for anything she did, but for keeping the confidences of her friends, which made her a sharer in their sins. When someone got caught and told on everyone, or snitched, great mercy was shown to that person; but great consequences came to those that were left exposed. The person that snitched could've been the biggest influencer in the group, maybe even the ringleader; the ideas and schemes most likely came from that individual, but if he/she sang like a canary to the elders? That person would more than likely be deemed repentant and allowed to remain in the congregation, getting full spiritual healing or stitches. The individuals that were exposed? The harshest punishment was reserved for hiding their sin. There were no secrets allowed. Privacy was a gift that no one was graced with.

There was always punishment for sin, and most of it was public. At the minimum, an announcement would be made to the entire congregation at the Thursday meeting that "the matter involving (blank) has been handled"; a sermon or public reproof talk would ensue, giving full details of the gross sin and the scriptural basis to back it up. Scriptures would be plucked from the Bible, some out of context, to support the reproof. There were also privileges taken away. Participation in the meetings would be restricted until you proved you were trustworthy again. The maximum sentence? Disfellowshipping, removal from the congregation because the uncleanness was detrimental to the spiritual purity of the rest of the congregation. The elders took it upon themselves to act on God's behalf, executing their judgment as if it were God's. Regardless of the consequence, gossip would ensue as the details of one's mistakes were made public. Shame would pursue the sinner for years after; some never recovered.

After a large sweep of the congregation that included many announcements, reproof, and discipline, the congregation would move forward in their state of self-righteousness and spiritual superiority to the rest of the world. The elders would feel bold and proud wielding their spiritual power to keep the organization clean. This was all done in Jehovah's name, as if He himself had made the judgments and spoken the decisions.

There was one exception to this breach of confidentiality for the cleanness of the congregation: Any person who was accused or convicted of child abuse was protected. In the early days, there wasn't even so much as a whisper of misconduct within families. Any abuse—whether it be physical, sexual, or emotional—was considered a family matter.

There was a time, I remember, when my mom's best friend, our neighbor, had come over crying. They were talking in whispers, but I overheard some of the words. She discovered her husband had been sexually abusing her two daughters. I do not remember hearing specific details, but I know my mom's friend was devastated. Mom called my dad, an elder, into the room for help. The gist of his words? They shouldn't be discussing it; it was a judicial matter and warned them both that there could be disciplinary action if they continued to talk about it. The abuser was disfellowshipped for about a year and then reinstated (brought back) into the congregation with no warning to the rest of the clueless families within the congregation. There was never intervention from law enforcement of any kind. Those two girls were instructed not to speak of the behavior again and threatened with being disfellowshipped if they did.

That is what I grew up with, believing the lie that policing your friends and family is what God expected of you. I was taught that God reacted to your mistakes with judgment and punishment. I judged others and myself by those standards, always falling short and living in a constant state of disappointment in myself and others. This lie is still propagated in that organization today.

The truth is that God holds each of us accountable for ourselves. Jesus came to this earth and lived in the flesh. He knows of our sinful nature and loves us unconditionally anyway. We are valuable to Him. Love is the foundation of His sacrifice, not law. He is aware of everything we do before we do it. He knows our motive and tries to nudge us away from what isn't good for us before we act on it. When we sin, as we all do daily, He forgives and heals us through His inspired word in the Bible. He certainly doesn't need any one of us to tell Him what someone else did; He already knows! Most of all, more than likely, He already forgave. He didn't place any one person or organization on this earth to spiritually judge another.

> Jesus tells us "Do not judge, and you will
> not be judged. Do not condemn, and you
> will not be condemned. Forgive and you
> will be forgiven" (Luke 6:37 NIV).

It took me over forty years of living in that state of telling and being told on before I finally gave up and left that organization. It was one of the most difficult yet crucial decisions I have or will have to make in my life. Doing so meant leaving all but a small handful of my closest friends and family behind. I still fight the urge to judge myself and others humanly, which is harshly. But now I know, based on the Bible in its entirety, how wrong that really is. I feel so blessed now to have my eyes opened to who God really is and the loving sacrifice Jesus gave for our sins.

CHAPTER 5

Induction into the Hall of Shame

These next few chapters will be hard to write; they may even be equally hard for some to read. The highs are high, the lows are the lowest: the result of believing in an organization that is not based on Jesus's love but rather on laws and rules—legalism.

The congregation we were in for the first eleven years of my life was well-stocked with elders, and the congregation fifteen miles away was not. Eureka was growing so large they needed to divide the congregation there into two. But when this request was submitted to their governing body in New York (the top tier of their organization), the answer was no. The congregation was told they didn't have enough elders to do so. We lived in a little lumber town somewhere between both cities, so it was decided that our family would transfer to the Eureka congregation to help facilitate the division of that congregation into two.

We could not have predicted or prepared for the changes and challenges or division our family was about to face.

Within a few months, we seemed to be fitting in nicely. My mom had rekindled some old friendships and made new friends, and together, they encouraged her to get her driver's license and helped her to do so. She was in her forties and had never gotten it. My sisters and I were all making new friends our age too, an indulgence we didn't have in our old congregation. We started to host get-togethers and got invited out to other parties as well. We seemed to be popular and well-liked as a family. For the first time in our lives, we were all happy and having *fun* together.

One of the friends my dad made was financially comfortable. He owned a janitorial business and quickly offered my mom a part-time job cleaning in the evenings for extra money. My mom now had a car and a job with her own money. She was beginning to look and act differently; she was gaining confidence. Mom would take each of my sisters and me on different nights to help with the jobs, and we started earning our own money as well. Money had always been tight for even the fundamentals, like clothing and shoes. We now had money to buy clothes and go do things with friends; we, too, were growing into confident young women. I was twelve when I realized there was freedom in earning my own money.

At the same time, my parents began fighting more often and with vigor. My sisters and I would sit on each other's beds at night, listening as the fights escalated louder and louder. We could hear objects hit the walls and, sometimes, what sounded like bodies. We would comfort each other, almost bonding over the trauma. To the world, we looked so together as a family. In reality, we were living with secrets, shame, and destructive dysfunction.

Dad worked rotating shifts. During this time, when he worked swing shift, some of my mom's new friends would come over and bring beer. We would play Forty-fives and dance and laugh. This was my introduction to partying. My young mind began to see that no matter how bad things were, a few beers could cure it. In time, these new friends seemed to show up every time my dad went to work. Drinking became more frequent, and so did some questionable behavior. I had no idea it was wrong, just that it was different. But we were all laughing, and I was allowed to be frisky; her friends actually encouraged it, so I loved our new life.

My dad was becoming quiet and distant. What we couldn't know was that my dad was struggling in his role as elder in our new congregation with the tenured group of men he was sent to help. There was a way they liked to handle matters, and my dad sometimes challenged that. There was one elder, the alpha, that had a strong hand of influence within the entire congregation. In hindsight, I think he felt threatened by my dad's opinions, combined with the acceptance we quickly received as a family in general. From the time we arrived, he looked for ways to demean my dad and bring our entire family out as unclean and bad association. He had a reputation for finding who he felt was the root of sin in the congregation and cutting it out, quietly being referred to as the Hatchet Man in some circles. He governed the congregation with rules and laws with no expressions of mercy, grace, or love. Oddly enough, he seemed to really respect and protect the new friends we had met. They engaged in questionable behavior, true, but he seemed okay with it. Looking back, I think in some way this validated them and their actions as godly in my young eyes.

Within a few months, secrets started to come out. Some inappropriate behavior was happening behind closed doors, and my mom was at the center of it, as were our new friends. So in line with the fundamental beliefs of the organization, my dad had my mom go to the elders and confess it all. From that point on, our new friends weren't welcome in our home anymore. The fun had come to a screeching halt, and a bleak sadness replaced it. My dad was angry and resentful that his family had sullied his reputation. Now he was faced with losing his coveted role as elder. My mom was heartbroken. She was mourning her freedom and friends as they were instructed to stay away from each other. My sisters and I had had a taste of excitement and fun, and now the house was still and quiet, except for the sobs coming from my mother's room. She would stay there for days. Sometimes, one of my sisters would call an old family friend for help. She would drive over and go into my mom's room for hours, trying to help her see the blessings she had out in her living room.

I don't know how long it took, but sooner or later, my mom was feeling better. Mom would dress in her cutoff jeans and flannel shirt, comb her hair, do her makeup, and go for long drives. We didn't know where she went, but she came home in good spirits, so we didn't ask questions either.

Within weeks, we found out she was meeting up with the forbidden friends, a huge no-no. Back to the elders she went, and this time, they dealt harshly with her and, consequently, my family. The Hatchet Man finally had the ammunition he needed to expose my family. My dad was stripped of his title as elder, and my mom was publicly reproved—an announcement read to the entire congregation, and a talk was delivered to the congregation of two hundred–plus outlining the torrid details of her behavior. The entire family was expected to sit through all of it with our heads down to show our repentance and acceptance of Jehovah's discipline. I cannot begin to describe the shame each of us felt. I had never felt this degradation and humiliation before. I didn't want to be there or ever come back again. But where are you going to go when you are disgraced and shamed from God?

Our family was broken, and in my adolescent mind, I believed it was our fault. God had spoken. He had disciplined us for having fun...hadn't he?

My mom started being medicated for anxiety and depression. My oldest sister plugged her headphones into her stereo and rocked in a chair to music for hours every day. My dad began to work all the overtime he could and wasn't present physically or emotionally any longer, bitter at the disgrace his family had brought him. He blamed us openly for the loss of his privilege of being an elder.

But the little frisky girl in me wanted the fun to return. All the parties had stopped, and with them, the laughter and dancing.

Ironically, there was leftover alcohol in the refrigerator door, but no friends came over to drink it. I started to sneak sips of leftover wine in the fridge or liquor in the cabinet to rekindle the feeling of liveliness that was long gone. To cover my tracks, I would fill the bottles up with just the right amount of water after each drink so no one would notice any disappearing liquid. When my mom would go into her room and close the door to cry and sleep the afternoon away, I would sneak out to the neighbor kids' houses. Again, the neighbor kids were forbidden because they were worldly, not part of the religion. But under the influence of a drink or two I had, I would crack jokes and be the life of the party, simulating the fun that was missing in our lives. But even under the influence, I was never fully able to overcome the disgrace I felt from those announcements, the whispers of the self-righteous friends that followed, and the heaviness in the house that couldn't be shaken.

Our weekly family Bible studies continued. We were even less engaged as Dad went through the motions of leading us from one book to another, never addressing the elephant in the room, the sin, consequent shame, and depression that was felt by all his girls and his wife. Although my dad prayed with the family in a routine and generic way, he never prayed specifically for his family and what we were going through. I'm not sure he believed in praying that way. But I believe, most of the time, he was disillusioned and ashamed of the family he felt he was stuck with.

During this time, I had developed a crush on an older boy that was working in the town that summer. I would follow him around and watch him work, flirting and giggling the whole time. It was innocent enough. But when he talked to me, I felt a warm buzz like the feeling of alcohol. I was happy and excited when he was around. Since the announcement, the positive male attention was now missing in my life. That attention was short-lived, however, when one of my besties, whose parents didn't have all the restrictions around her social life that I did, caught his eye; and they began dating. I watched as her flirting and giggling garnered his attention. I was no longer of any interest to him.

Typical pubescent drama, true, but it impacted me severely. As the darkness from the family shame crept in, I felt rejected, defeated, and worthless. I tried to counter it by chugging wine out of the refrigerator door, but now, the heaviness remained. There was no one to share my feelings with without being outed and judged. The mere act of having interest in the opposite sex would be deemed a sin. Talking about my feelings and actions could lead someone, anyone, to feel the need to report me to the elders, which I absolutely couldn't face. And God? I had been taught to believe He had turned His face away from me the minute I pursued that boy. I had no one, and I was drowning in my teenage emotions and feelings.

That is when I decided I needed to exit the pain. After an afternoon of a few drinks and no relief, I saw my mom's purse open on the dining room chair with all her prescription bottles whispering, "Just take us." I reached in, pulled out each bottle, and took her pills. I went upstairs, took off my little silver ring I had on so that no one would have to take it off my dead body (dramatic, I know), crawled into a ball, and drifted off into a cloud, floating up to a space with no darkness, only light. I felt nothing, and it felt great!

The next thing I remember is yelling and tugging at me. My parents discovered I had passed out, which quickly led to my mom looking in her purse and discovering what I had done. They loaded me up into the car and drove me to the emergency room at the local hospital. I was in and out of consciousness, but somehow, they communicated to me that one of the elders was waiting in the lobby. Attempting to take my life was a sin, they told me; this was going to result in a judicial committee matter when this was all over. That was all I needed to know to clench my jaw and refuse to drink the ipecac the hospital staff was trying to administer. I absolutely didn't want to live to face more judgment, more disapproval. That is when the tube went up my nose and down my throat to pump my stomach. I cried and choked for the next few hours. When the doctors believed I was out of danger, they sent me home with a prescription for charcoal and two very disappointed parents. That night, as I clutched the toilet basin, vomiting, my mom came into the bathroom; wet a washcloth; and put it on my head as I told her I was so sorry. There was the shame and guilt again. I couldn't apologize enough.

Mom leaned down and said, "Oh, sweetie! Don't be sorry. You stopped me from doing this myself." My mom, too, was feeling the darkness that encompassed our home! I looked up at her with a combination of responsibility, guilt, and sadness. Those feelings would come in waves for years after that.

We had transferred back to the small congregation in Arcata, a shell of a family. We were immersed in the old congregation filled with conservative friends from times past. But now, they looked at us with apprehension, almost concerned that we were tainted to a level that could be contagious.

The first order of congregation business was to discipline me for my blatant act of disregard for my life, which was a grave sin. There I was, this broken thirteen-year-old, and they were reading scriptures to me from the Old Testament about God's view of taking a life, even your own. Shame, shame, shame! I was put on private reproof. If no one found out what happened, they wouldn't have to make an announcement to the entire congregation…this time.

My dad received a form in the mail from the hospital that required both of our signatures, confirming I was receiving proper mental health help, aftercare. He took me into the living room, had me read it, and said, "Do you see what you did? You caused a lot of problems for your dad. Now we need to sign this and send it back to them."

When I protested—I mean, we hadn't done any aftercare, and secretly, I really wanted help—he said, "Yes, we did. We took you to the elders."

There are many moments since then that I have felt that doomed feeling of guilt and shame. Like many teens, I made a lot of bad choices (see the next few chapters) and suffered natural consequences of them.

The lie I believed for years is that it was God lowering His head in embarrassment regarding my decisions and behavior. There was no help from Him. I was on my own to figure it out, and I should come back to talk to Him once I had. But I can now say with confidence that

God isn't holding my mistakes over my head like a countdown to strike three. He is there for me, for you, to help get through these moments, even if they are self-induced. It has taken me years to fully understand that shame is not of God.

The truth is, nowhere in God's inspired word will you read of our powerful God using His power to shame those who have sinned to the point of the sinner feeling hopeless. That is not who He is. It is so important to understand His love for us even at our worst because it is that love that keeps us from shaming, not only others but ourselves as well.

And the elders in the congregations of the world that wield their power like hatchets? What does the Bible really say God's expectations are for them?

> "Are any of you sick? You should call the elders of the church to come and pray over you, anointing you with oil in the name of the Lord. Such a prayer offered in faith will heal the sick, and the Lord will make you well. And if you have committed any sins, you will be forgiven" (James 5:14 NLT)

Those are inspired words of instruction from God on how He wants our sin handled. It is very clear. Go to the elders for God's healing, and "you will be forgiven."

"The Lord is merciful and gracious, slow
to anger and abounding in steadfast love.
He will not always chide, nor will he keep
his anger forever. He does not deal with us
according to our sins, nor repay us according to our iniquities. For as high as the
heavens are above the earth, so great is his
steadfast love toward those who fear him;
as far as the east is from the west, so far
does he remove our transgressions from
us." (Psalm 103:8–12 ESV)

This is David speaking from his own place of recovery
from his mistakes, explaining how God sees it. These are
inspired words of instruction from God on how He wants
our sin and sadness to be handled.

Although I had access to both of those scriptures, I
allowed myself to believe they were only true within the
confines of the elders, who they chose to help and who they
chose to eliminate. It would be many years before I read
those words and knew they were from God to me.

CHAPTER 6

Two Lives Are Better Than None

Like most girls, I wanted to be accepted and feel good about myself even in a time when there is so much change such as adolescence. In most households, this is a challenge. In my house, this was an intense conflict every day. I had to make a choice—be accepted by my family/church/God, or be accepted with school/friends/self...or did I?

After the suicide attempt, my mom realized we all needed an outlet for exercise. A gym that was locally owned in the area ran a special for an annual membership for the entire family that was too good to pass up. In an attempt to lift the dark haze in our home, Mom convinced Dad to ante up the money for the membership (something he did infrequently unless a shiny electronic for his collection was the object). So as a family, we began going to the gym. At first, the 6:00 a.m. alarm was a source of complete angst. But then, Mom introduced me to the owner; and he became my personal trainer, confidant, and object of my affection (aka, obsession). This also began my love of physical activity, which continues to this day.

Within weeks, I discovered my natural ability to develop muscle and strength. My new friend was impressed and showed me off as his newest protégé to all the regulars at the gym. To your average teenage girl, of course, that would be exciting, but to one that hadn't gotten any positive attention or accolades in months, this was addicting. My parents welcomed the man into our circle even though he wasn't one of us or of our religion. This was unheard of in our religion at that time, but he was relieving my parents of the stress of parenting a frisky teenage girl, so it was an exception worth the risk in their minds...a mistake they probably regret to this day.

I became obsessed with my workouts, my gains, and my mentor.

It wasn't long before the inappropriateness began, however. The hugs would linger a few seconds longer than they should. A grope of my backside when no one was looking. Long-winded phone calls that ended with his words stabbing me: "If only you were a few years older." I was fourteen.

I would do anything to gain his approval. He needed a babysitter so he could go on a date? I would drop everything, even long-standing obligations with my regular gigs (this resulted in the loss of my reliability = being fired = loss of that spending money). He needed someone to do his books? I quickly learned data entry and did months of backlogging of his bills and income. These are my earliest memories of being a people pleaser, doing anything to make someone happy at my own expense.

There were several in the gym that saw what was going on and tried to warn my parents. You see, this man had had several inappropriate relationships with young girls in the club; I wasn't the first. My parents brought this up to me, and I laughed it all off, making up a benign relationship. "He's like an uncle," I would tell them. I would then double down on the participation at meetings, go door-to-door with more vigor than ever and be joyfully submissive to my parents and the church. All the evidence would point my parents away from the danger. This man was thirty-one after all. "What interest could he possibly have with a four-teen-year-old child," they would say.

In time, his business could not stay afloat, and the gym closed. I was devastated. I was in high school and had access to weights in PE, and that helped. I called him every day, sometimes several times a day at his new job selling cars, and we would talk for hours. He would proclaim his love to me but tell me it had to remain a secret because people wouldn't understand. I completely agreed; news of this would certainly garner disapproval, even possibly more congregation announcements. I didn't want to face any more public condemnation.

He had his own shame of a failed business, and soon enough, he decided to run away from it all and moved out of the area. I was devastated. I cried for weeks and hardly ate. My parents were irritated by the adolescent drama and decided I had gotten off balance, and I needed to refocus my dedication to Jehovah God. This is when the conversations began for me to think about getting baptized; it was time for me to stand on my own with God. I told my friend on one of our phone calls about the pressure. He agreed with my parents and said getting baptized could be a fresh start for me and cleanse both of us of our guilt. I would do anything for his approval, including taking this monumental step.

In this faith, although I was being raised as a member of the congregation and the threat of condemnation from men who spoke for God was ever-present, discipline was less permanent or severe. Once baptized, however, even simple teenage shenanigans that broke their rules would be dealt with severely, up to and including removal from the congregation, disfellowshipped.

The process of baptism is not as basic and simple as saying and believing the salvation prayer with a symbolic water baptism shortly after. No, in this religion, there are a rigorous series of questions that the one wanting to be baptized answers with two elders over several sessions. They refer to it as going over the questions.

Next, they all meet and decide whether you are ready for baptism, and you are either granted permission to do so at the next assembly/convention, or you are told you must wait. Most people are excited to be taking this next step and talk about it. But that is a mistake because if you are told you aren't ready by the elders and not seen getting baptized at that next assembly/convention, then the whispers begin circulating throughout the congregation. This is when questions were raised, and tongues would wag as to why the approval wasn't given.

One of my sessions was held in my bedroom. My room was typical of a young girl. I was obsessed with muscles and working out, so of course, my bedroom walls were lined with glossy photos of various bodybuilders, male and female alike. Nothing was mentioned to me about my décor, nor was I asked why I was so fascinated with these images during this session. But after all the sessions were complete, my parents were invited to take me to the backroom of the church for a meeting. At this meeting, the elders expressed concern over my bedroom décor. They read scriptures to support how wrong the obsession with exercise was (1 Timothy 4:8, particularly, "Bodily training is beneficial for a little; but godly devotion is beneficial for all things," their version).

In view of what they believed the Bible to say about this matter, they gave me their decision; I would need to reveal what was in my heart by receiving their counsel, remove all the pictures from my walls, and quit obsessing about exercise, showing them godly devotion was my priority. They told me this would prove I was worthy of baptism. In hindsight, I, of course, can see how absurd and wrong their procedures are. How our heavenly Father must cringe at the obstacle course laid out for those that want to come to Him. The arrogance of men that feel they speak for God as to who can/can't get baptized! But at the time, I saw it as an obstacle course I had to not only run through but excel at in order to be accepted by God.

So yet another step up the ladder of saying whatever needed to be said to have the best of both of my worlds. I convinced them I had no attachments to those posters or that lifestyle. I committed to leaving that back room, going home, and taking down all the pictures immediately. They gave the approval to be baptized into their organization at the next circuit assembly in the spring. I remember being so sad as I took each of those pictures off the walls, careful not to tear them up. The white walls left behind looked so barren and cold. I wondered how this made any difference to God, but then I realized I didn't understand Him, so I had to trust the elders and my parents with that.

The first few months after my baptism were full of peace and happiness in our home. Soon, my parents purchased our first home, and we moved to Eureka. We spent the next few months settling back into the Eureka congregation again.

The fear of man was also settling into our home. My parents were both trying to rebuild their reputation to get my dad's privileges back. The Hatchet Man was still in full control of the congregation, which made my parents extremely nervous. As soon as we began attending the new congregation, my parents gave us a stern warning: *Do not do anything that will put you in the back room with these elders!* We all knew we would be judged severely. My two sisters and I were now baptized, which meant we would be subject to the harshest of judgments, disfellowshipped, or removed from the congregation.

I was now highly adept at hiding who I was and what I was doing from any that would disapprove. I was dating behind my parents' back. I was even occasionally sneaking out of the house as soon as everyone went to sleep and returning at dawn. Sleeping in until noon was excused as "she's a teenager." Little did they know, every few weeks, I was being picked up by my twenty-year-old crush, drinking, having sex, and being dropped off before anyone woke up. How could they know? In between nights out, I was throwing myself into meetings, participating with the kind of enthusiasm that almost seemed bipolar. I regularly signed up to auxiliary pioneer, which required sixty hours a month of door-to-door, balancing that with my schoolwork (straight As, of course) and my secret life activities. To the onlookers, I seemed to be the perfect Christian example of living the best, clean life. To my inner circle of friends and the sister that I shared a room with, the disgust at my hypocrisy was beginning to leave a most undesirable taste in their mouth.

As for myself? I didn't even know who I was anymore.

One evening a few weeks after I had gotten my driver's license, the older man from the gym called and was in town, reappearing after a year of silence and absence. I was now sixteen, and he was thirty-three. He came to the house, and my parents greeted him with open arms. After the niceties were exchanged, I convinced my parents to let me take him for a drive with my parents' car and my new driver's license. Once out of their sight, we pulled over on a side street and started kissing. The excitement and passion were intense. We made a plan for me to sneak out that night and meet him down the road. He would take care of the rest.

The rest doesn't need to be written; it goes without saying what happened that night. I was only intimate with that man once in my life. It had been months since I had been with anyone, including my crush. Although I had always been told (as we all try to tell our kids now), it only takes one act of intimacy to change the trajectory of your life, I didn't believe it. But I am a living example of that being true with 100 percent certainty.

Afterward, he dropped me off with promises to keep in touch. I was ecstatic for a few days, on a hormone high. But that was short-lived.

His calls never came; he disappeared. Within weeks the reality of what I had done sank in, I was pregnant. I tried to ignore it at first. I mean, I had been quite success-ful at living two lives up until this point; maybe by mir-acle I could still manage these lives. I tried to call him to tell him, and his phone number was disconnected. He was gone once again, without a trace. What I didn't know then, but would find out soon, was that he had moved in with his ex-wife and was trying to reconcile with her at the time of our rendezvous.

A mutual friend of his and mine, a woman in her forties became my go-to for information and advice. She was the go-between as he tried to separate himself from his sin and, in effect, me. I would go to her house when I was supposed to be at school, and she would let me cry on her shoulder. I didn't know that while I was confiding my innermost fears to her, she was his confidant as well; she was playing both sides. At first, she told me he felt it was someone else's baby, suggesting that if I kept the baby, I should tell people it was the boy that he knew I had snuck out with prior. That stung! Not only had I not been with that boy in weeks but we also had always used birth control.

I was living in this fantasy that I could marry this older man, have the baby, convince the elders I was repentant, and keep my family and friends from the church in my life.

The day came for me to go to the clinic to find out my birthing options. This mutual friend acted as if she was my biggest supporter and insisted on taking me. It was at this appointment she so innocently asked the clinician, "What about abortion? When is that no longer an option?" I was shocked, taken completely off guard. Did she not have confidence in me as a woman to be a good mom? In a state of confusion, I took all the information from the clinic counselor and followed my friend to her car. In the car, she said, "I think this is a good option, and you should entertain it."

For the next hour, she pleaded her case; my parents would never know what had happened, and therefore, I could go about my life with no consequences. She would contact the man, and he would come into town and take care of the whole thing, financially and emotionally. She knew that the last piece of the plan was going to be the most appealing to me because, at this point, he had not been taking my calls, there had been no direct communication, and he had completely abandoned me. If I didn't get the abortion? He would go to jail for having sex with a minor, and I would be left raising a baby by myself because my parents would probably kick me out of their home and life.

In that moment, I was brought back into reality. That brought me back down to earth, so to speak, and I hit the ground hard. I had no other option according to her. As this religion is ready to judge and remove, I had no one else to talk to without damnation.

This is the decision I can never take back. I regretted it from the minute I allowed it to be an option. It has plagued and haunted me constantly since. I decided to take her advice.

The date of the procedure was set for two weeks later. He came up, took me to the clinic, paid, and sat in the waiting room with me. After the procedure, he left, taking with him the hopes and dreams of a sixteen-year-old girl.

I tried to live extra from that day on. Extra participation within the church. Extra close to home, no sneaking out, no drinking. Extra exercising, taking long walks, at which time I pleaded with God for forgiveness, not believing for a second I was deserving of it.

Around this time, I started dating a man ten years older than me. He was in the same faith, so it was accepted. He brought fun and laughter back into my life and showered me with love letters and compliments. Dating was not to be taken lightly in this organization. Dating is reserved for the sole purpose of getting to know each other and getting married. Dating is not to be used as a developmental tool in the transition from youth to adult and is not allowed recreationally. When this was brought up to him, he pronounced his love and intention to my parents, and we started talking about getting married.

During this time, for the first time in my life, I was consumed with praying, begging God not to make me go to the elders about what had happened and the gross sin that I had committed. I remember many times while doing laps on the track during PE pleading with God for a sense of redemption, a clean conscience. In those moments, in hindsight, God was with me. He knew my heart and was trying to hold me and comfort me. But I still held tight to the concept of forgiveness only coming from the elders within the congregation. So I didn't allow the intimacy with God in the stillness of those moments, I didn't think it was possible with such a dirty, tainted girl like me.

The small group of girlfriends that I had confided in saw me moving on in a good way and got angry, maybe even envious. They constantly reminded me of my secret sin-filled past, threatening to reveal my sins to the elders if I became self-righteous.

One night, a talk was given at the meeting regarding not keeping any secrets from the elders. There was an example given of a woman who worked in the medical transcription field who came across a doctor's dictation that involved a member of the congregation having an abortion. In this story, the woman had to go to the elders and tell all she knew knowing she was breaking several laws and would lose her job to be obedient to Jehovah. The moral of the story? All sin must be exposed to the elders regardless of the cost to someone's HEPA rights. My girlfriends heard this and held their secret no more. I felt convicted and ashamed after the meeting and tried to leave as soon as the meeting was over. But they caught me in the parking lot. The girls told me it was time to go back inside and come clean. They even escorted me back into the church under the guise that they would support me through it.

With tears streaming down my face, I grabbed two elders and took them into the back room and spilt the horribleness darkening my conscience. My sobs were the only sound that filled the silence that followed. I was crying so hard that when they got my dad and brought him into the backroom, they had to tell him what I had confessed. I was too emotional to even speak. The only words out of his mouth were "Well, she lied to us then."

You see, a few weeks after the procedure, a letter had come to the house from the abortion clinic with the results of my first pelvic exam and subsequent pap smear. My dad got the letter and confronted me with it. Horrified, I had told them I went to the clinic because my periods were heavy, and I was too ashamed to tell them. My dad believed my lie and paid the bill. But now that he knew the truth first, he was in shock, but then, he was too angry and disgusted to look at me, let alone comfort me.

It was months before he even looked in my direction again. Even if he had to talk to me, he looked at the ground or the space behind me.

In the next few weeks, my life unraveled.

Several elders' meetings culminated in the decision to disfellowship me. My middle sister who was aware of my secret life but held my confidence was also disfellowshipped for not turning me in months before. She had then been blamed for my pregnancy because, according to them, if she had come forward the first time I snuck out, none of this would've happened. My dad retreated deeper into himself once again, pitying himself for having such unclean worldly daughters that he would probably never be an elder again. My girlfriends showed themselves disloyal opportunists using my shame to step up into congregation social circles, deflecting any of the hiding and lying they were involved in. They told my shameful secret to anyone who would listen under the guise of needing to talk to someone about this heavy burden, my secret sin.

The dense, dark cloud had descended on our household once again.

The lie was pounded into my head: "You are bad because you sinned!" and "You sin. We find out. You are contagious, so we remove you because you are evil." There was even speculation then and now that I have committed the ultimate unforgivable sin in God's eyes. Some of you reading this may even wonder the same. That's between you and God. I wrestled with that question for decades.

But when I am in prayer, reading God's words to me, I know those are untruths now.

> "The Lord our God is merciful and forgiving, even though we have rebelled against him." (Daniel 9:9 NIV)

> "How can I know all the sins lurking in my heart? Cleanse me from these hidden faults. Keep your servant from deliberate sins! Don't let them control me. Then I will be free of guilt and innocent of great sin." (Psalm 19:12, 13 NLT)

The truth is, God sees us the way we really are. He knows what we do in public and what we are trying to hide. We can bring it all to Him shamelessly because He already knows. God knows what's in your heart more than you do and invites you to seek it out with Him. He has no expectations of perfection or faultlessness. He knows we are weak and sinful; and He wants us to approach Him, look for Him, and walk with Him…always and in all ways.

If I had known that then, maybe the next thirty years could've been spent serving Him. Instead, this began my journey of striving after the approval of men, believing that is how I would attain the approval of God.

CHAPTER 7

Sorry You're Not Sorry

The next few weeks were full of consequences. I told the man I was dating that I needed to come clean to the elders about something I had been concealing if we were to have a life together with God in it. He was extremely supportive, but he had no idea the seriousness of what I had done. He only knew me to be bubbly and spiritually minded. In hindsight, I think he couldn't have imagined that I had lived such a double life and thought the disfellowshipping would be a brief few months after which we would resume our life together.

As the night of the announcement drew closer, he sent me gifts professing his love, including a small, gold promise ring.

It was during this time that it was insinuated that high school had been the source of my bad conduct. It was at school that I had done most of my lying and sneaking. After all, school had been the only place I had any freedom. The decision was made to drive over to Redding to take the

GED, putting an end to high school, get a part-time job, and begin working full time at showing my repentance.

It was on this visit that the man I was dating told me he would wait for me, and we became committed.

Arriving home from that three-hour trek, I had hope and a plan. I was sorry, so sorry, for the double life I had led. I knew then, as I do now, the gravity of my mistakes. I longed to do and be better than those sins I committed. I wanted to earn back the love and trust of my parents, the friends in the congregation, and of course, the elders who had the power to reinstate me.

Within a few weeks, however, the weight of my sin was beginning to feel immensely heavy. There was so much shame and blame in my home. Many nights, my parents could be heard loudly discussing in the next room what my middle sister and I had done to the family. The loneliness and isolation left a large, empty space inside, and I had no idea what to do with it. There were no tools to cope, and I was misled to believe God was not accessible at this point. I started to eat excessively, binging on anything and everything, trying to fill my heart and soul.

My middle sister became my new best friend as we were both disfellowshipped, trying to be reinstated, and there was no one else that would associate with us. It was a relationship built on necessity, although the underlying bitterness she felt for being in this state because of me was looming over us every moment we were together.

Coming out of winter, figuratively and literally, was hard. We enrolled together in trade classes, typing, and computers. I began getting up at 6:00 a.m. doing exercise classes in the living room with whichever instructor was on TV that morning. My day consisted of early rising to exercise, our classes, a part-time job from 3:00 to 6:00 p.m. and home to study for the meetings.

Regular meeting attendance was one of the main ways that repentance would be shown, which was the key to being forgiven and allowed back into the organization.

In these months, shame was present constantly.

Although going to the meetings was required, no one was allowed to talk to you; even smiling your direction was frowned upon. I have heard recently that this policy has changed. Nowadays, a disfellowshipped person may be greeted and acknowledged at the meetings unless that same group of men, the elders, deems them to be an apostate. Apostates, anyone who dares question or believe outside of their teachings, are considered dangerous, and therefore, no association whatsoever is allowed.

During the meetings where there were question-and-answer sessions, the microphone carriers would be looking at whatever book/tract/magazine we were all currently studying to see if ours were underlined or studied as they passed the microphone to someone nearby. The spies were everywhere, looking for something to report. News of my vile sin had spread, and many didn't want me to be allowed back into the congregation, ever. There were nights that I was so sick with a cold or flu (pre-COVID obviously) but went to the meetings anyway because missing them would be a sign of unrepentance, which could be time added onto your sentence.

So I would arrive and walk in as the opening song began and try to find the seat closest to the back, hopefully in a corner, leaving as soon as the last amen was uttered. Lingering before or after was not only extremely uncomfortable but was also a sign of rebelliousness, which wouldn't bode well for you when it came time to apply for reinstatement.

Being home was not particularly comfortable either. Not only was Dad disgusted and angry, but my sister and I weren't allowed to eat at the same time as our family. If my parents had a dinner party or anyone came to visit, we had to remove ourselves from the room so as not to make the visitor uncomfortable by our disfellowshipped presence. The scripture in 1 Corinthians 5:11 was used to show this was from God. Their version read, "But now I am writing you to quit mixing in company with anyone called a brother that is a fornicator or a greedy person or an idolator or a reviler or a drunkard or an extortioner, not even eating with such a man." There it was plainly written, no more family dinners. We were outcast from our own dining rooms; I was sixteen.

When enough time has passed, you are allowed to write a letter to the body of elders requesting a meeting to discuss reinstatement. On the sixth month, I wrote my first letter. The response? My sin was so gross that they wouldn't even contemplate meeting with me until I had been out at least a year! Their response hit hard. I felt set back and unsure I would ever be forgiven by God.

As I sat in my room at night studying every written word in their literature, I was motivated by the perseverance of my own DNA because I felt no connection to God, let alone any redemption from Jesus. I had only the coldness of being in the shadow of everyone's back that was turned because I was sorry but not sorry enough.

Now let's talk about the man I was committed to but had no direct communication with during this time. The relationship was now fueled by the smallest of crumbs. I had, of course, his ring; and he had mine, showing our commitment to each other. Because of that, he was involved in our family. My oldest sister had gotten engaged, and he was asked to be a part of the wedding party. There were weekly phone calls between him and my mom, which I was allowed to silently listen to on the other line. He wasn't allowed to use my name, so he would ask how everyone was. The weekly recap of my activities and all I had done or not done would be relayed. When the matter of my weight came up, my mom told him I had been depressed and gained some weight.

His quick response was, "I'm not going to be with someone that is fat and sloppy."

Mom assured him I was exercising and working hard at getting back in shape. After every phone call, I felt so good, an emotional high. But within a few days I would hear his words echo in my head and grow so anxious about my weight. My workouts were intense, but the emptiness was even more intense. This is when the binging and attempt at purging began. I used laxatives and extreme exercise after each episode of binging because I couldn't be "fat and sloppy."

The body-shaming and the threat of abandonment if I put on five pounds have never left me. I continue to struggle with food addiction and body image. Seeing myself through God's eyes is a daily challenge.

Fast-forward to my sister's wedding.

There were family and friends coming from out of town, and our house was going to be full; therefore, the two disfellowshipped members of the family were asked to go elsewhere. We had to book, pay for, and stay at a hotel away from the festivities. The man I was engaged to was assigned to stay in my room, and we secretly left notes in a journal I put out on my dresser. Again, any direct contact would be a violation of the disfellowshipped state and could be cause for severe discipline to us both. My other sister and I were allowed to go to the wedding but not allowed to speak to anyone or go to the reception. The reason? The Kingdom Hall is a public building open to anyone, and the reception would be at a private recreation hall with the option to make it closed to those who were bad association (i.e., the disfellowshipped people).

The wedding was beautiful. My oldest sister was stunning. Caught up in the beauty of it all, my middle sister and I drove back to our hotel room feeling conflicted. On the one hand, we were happy for our oldest sister, such a big day for her, and it had all turned out so beautifully. On the other hand, we were clearly not wanted there, outcasts of our own family because of our sin that we felt so sorry for.

As the months became a year, I wrote another letter to the elders, asking for a meeting for reinstatement. Coincidentally, my fiancé's mother also decided to come from Redding for a visit around this same time and brought with her a young woman from Redding to keep her company. I was granted a meeting with the elders, and that meeting was scheduled on one of the nights she was staying with us, and I couldn't be any more ecstatic! I envisioned the meeting going well, resulting in my reinstatement into the organization and coming home to celebrate altogether.

The day of the meeting, I thought about all the things I would point out as proof of how sorry I was. Walking into that meeting I thought I was well prepared and ready to plead my case.

The meeting was a disaster.

The Hatchet Man had done his preparation as well and was determined more than ever that I wasn't going to be a part of the congregation again. He referred in detail to all my previous sins and deceit as his evidence of my permanent uncleanness. When he spoke of the abortion, he told me it was a sin so bad I had no way to understand how bad it was on this side of Armageddon. He told me I could pray for God to help me forgive myself and relieve the pain as I grew older, but he doubted even that would be possible. There was even a moment in the meeting that he and Dad went toe to toe as he attacked my dad verbally. He pointed out his discernment years ago that my dad was a bad shepherd; and the state of his children was clear evidence, according to him, that he was correct. It became clear that not only was I not going to be reinstated, but this vendetta between my dad and this man was also being played out at my expense.

We left the meeting overwhelmed with emotion. We spent the next hour at home teetering back and forth from crying to yelling. We were all a combination of angry and yet disillusioned at the same time. Little did I know, our house guest was hanging on every word from her bedroom. I found out months later that she had called her son the next day to tell him there had to be more going on for me not to be reinstated. I must be hiding something else. In her opinion, a disfellowshipped person would never be left outside of their organization for this amount of time otherwise.

On the three-hour drive home, she began her plot to free her son from me by encouraging a relationship between her female travel companion and her son. Once home, she told her son to take down all my pictures. I was a sinner, and she wouldn't have that up in her home (yes, he still lived at home with his mama). The next weekly phone call between my mom and him was very different. He was distant, there was suspicion in his questions, and he began to insinuate that possibly I was playing him, out gallivanting while he was pining away for me, waiting patiently for my return to the congregation. My mom tried to reason with him that there was more going on that she couldn't discuss, but he didn't believe her.

I should've realized I had lost him as the phone calls became sporadic and spaced out. But I held onto the hope that I could fix this once I was reinstated.

Three months later, I petitioned the elders again. The committee for judicial hearings is made up of three elders, and the majority typically rules. This time, the meeting was very different. As I spoke of how sorry I was once again, the other two men listened intently. After only a few minutes, my parents and I were asked to leave the room for the committee to deliberate. We waited outside for almost an hour before we were asked to rejoin them to hear my fate. This time, the other two elders stood up for me, citing that after fifteen months of loyally attending the meetings and respecting the disfellowshipped state, all while remaining clean, I was ready to be reinstated. The Hatchet Man gave a small speech in which he continued to accidentally use verbiage that suggested he was not in agreement. His words of doubt echoed in my head around every trial and temptation I endured for years to come.

A week later, a letter was read to the congregation that I was reinstated, and just like that, all were free to associate with me again. I waited for three days for my fiancé to call. He didn't. When I finally called him, he informed me he was not in love with me anymore. To say that proclamation affected me is an understatement. I was rocked. I would find out later that he was involved with someone else, the girl that came to visit with his mom. What had begun to heal in my heart was once again broken.

Soon, word got out that he was committed to me when he got involved with her, which was frowned upon. My mom called one of the elders in his congregation in Redding to officially report his betrayal. He was chastised privately for his lack of character, a small penance compared to what I had become accustomed to for my own missteps. The two of them got married but in a low-key, private ceremony. One of my friends was related to his new bride. She blamed me for their inability to have a big elaborate wedding in the church building and told my mom there was nothing wrong with what he had done. After all, "all is fair in love and war" (her words). This all happened within the confines of what is touted as a Christian organization.

The lie that forgiveness comes from God through an earthly group of men would haunt me and poison everything I thought about myself and God for years to come.

The truth is that when God forgives, He removes the sin from us. He wants us to let go and leave it at the altar. His forgiveness comes directly from His heart to yours, no middleman needed.

> "The sacrifice you desire is a broken spirit.
> You will not reject a broken and repentant
> heart" (Psalm 51:17 NLT).

When God sees us in our broken state of repentance, even if its self-inflicted through sin, He will not reject us. No one has the authority to do so, especially to do so as if they speak for God.

None of the shun or disapproval I endured, or anyone endures, is of God! He erased my sin the minute I came to him and confessed it. He removed it. He is the Almighty. He doesn't need any man here on earth to speak for Him. His words always get lost in translation when mankind tries.

CHAPTER 8

Forgiven but Never Forgotten

When you are reinstated, it is with full restrictions. In other words, everyone is now free to talk to you, but you are not free to fully participate in congregation privileges until you earn them back. So for the next few months, I would study and attend all the meetings but could not raise my hand to participate during the group discussions. I could go out in the ministry for unlimited number of hours, but I couldn't be a pioneer-official title for those that participate fifty hours or more a month. Although I had a close circle of friends that accepted me back with open arms, most of the congregation was encouraged to be cautious so as not to get influenced by any residual sin I may or may not be hanging onto still. Everyone needed time for me to prove that I was trustworthy.

The first six months, I can remember being full of gratitude to be included in any outings or activities because I had been isolated for so many months. Movie nights at the home of a dear old friend were especially fun. We watched chick flicks, ate good food, and gossiped a lot in between.

There seemed to be acceptance with this small group of women. Sure, we talked about any and everyone in the congregation (not so Christlike, for sure), but I really didn't give that a second thought because I was being included again. I must be okay in God's eyes if I was included.

In car groups out in the ministry, in between return visits (returning to speak to those we had left literature with prior), and working the not-at-homes (houses that had not answered the door on a previous day), there was more talking. Gossip, speculation, sharing feelings, and getting advice are all common and accepted ways to pass the time. In those months, I spent many hours in the ministry soaking up all the fellowship I could get. I literally felt starved of human interaction from the prior year.

It was in one of these car groups that I was shocked to hear mention of what had gotten me in trouble. I stared in disbelief as the driver, a pioneer, bluntly stated that it would be a long time before any brother (bachelor) would want anything to do with me because of my history of gross sin. The shame rushed through me like wildfire, burning all the new leaves of confidence blooming inside of me to the nubs. I asked her, "How would he know?"

She explained in a matter-of-fact way that it would be someone's Christian obligation to inform anyone that expressed interest in me that I had a history of sin. He would need to be warned of the potential of who he could be getting involved with. Stunned, I said no more in the car that day.

I had unanswered questions for God, but in my naivety, I didn't realize I could ask Him. Things like "How could

I have gone through all that I went through to prove I was sorry only to still be seen through the eyes of my past sin?" "When am I ever going to get beyond this?" "Will I ever be good enough for a mate, let alone God?"

Disillusioned, I began isolating myself from movie nights and the ministry.

After a few weeks, Mom could tell something had happened. I was deeply depressed and stayed home from the social outings, going only to meetings and my part-time job. Mom had started a little ritual after we were reinstated in which she made a cup of International Foods–flavored coffee (think instant lattes or mochas in a tin can), and we would sit and talk. She called it having a cup of chocolate together. I truly miss those moments to this day. I believe my mom was trying to be there for us, to reconnect that mother-daughter bond again. During our chocolate talks, I would open to Mom about my concerns. Mostly, she just listened, which was comforting.

One night, as we were driving home from work, I asked her if she thought I would ever find an eligible brother that would truly love me. Her words have echoed in my head for almost four decades: "I completely understand your worries. You and your sisters are ordinary girls that don't stand out in a crowd. It's going to be hard enough to find a mate based on that fact alone, not to mention you've been disfellowshipped already and you are only seventeen."

I do not believe my mom even knew the pain those words would scar me with for years. My mom is not a mean-spirited woman that would intentionally harm her daughter. In hindsight, I realize now that Mom had been trying to warn me of what was to come. She knew from her own experience in this religion what dating could be like for young women. She had already witnessed these brothers sift through the sisters (bachelorettes) as if they were panning for gold. She saw sisters spun around the pan by the brothers in the congregation like grains of sand, only to be cast down the river as worthless at the first sight of imperfection, as the men then dipped their pan back into the water looking for the perfect wife, their gold.

At this point, I joined another gym and was working out with weights as well as going to group exercise classes. I have always loved the gym atmosphere and knew I needed to do something to combat depression. By nature, I am a friendly person, and I quickly began to get to know the regulars, including the man at the front desk. He would greet patrons with a smile and encouraging words. Every new member was given a training program that he would walk you through one time and cheer you on from the front desk from then on. I had something new to look forward to four times a week (anything more was excessive; I was told by my congregation friends). I watched my body respond to the vigorous workouts and felt proud of myself for the first time in a long time. The regulars started weighing in "you should compete," referring to bodybuilding contests. I really wanted to, but when I brought the idea to my parents, there was disapproval and fear once again. After all, stripping down to a small bikini, oiling up, and performing on stage was not the modest behavior of a Christian.

I was going to all the meetings and going out in the ministry weekly, just not as wholeheartedly. My dad was still desperately trying to get back his elder title and jumped through every hoop put in front of him. His daughters were both reinstated now, and he was confident that any day, he would be asked to serve as a ministerial servant, one step down away from appointment as an elder.

There was a traveling overseer that would come through the area every few months. He was the person that would approve of any candidates recommended by the existing group of elders to be promoted to elevated positions, i.e., ministerial servants and elders. Typically, within four to six weeks of such a visit, an announcement would be made to the congregation, letting them know who had been approved by the group of men in New York that ran the organization.

After one of the meetings where the announcements were made and my dad was once again not one of the new appointees, Dad confronted the Hatchet Man and asked why he wasn't recommended. The Hatchet Man brought over another younger elder to back him up and went through an entire list of shortcomings my dad had, including, "Julia is secretly dating a worldly man from the gym!" My dad, indignant, sought me out in the building and took me to the two elders who were waiting in the very front of the hall by the stage, demanding to know who I was dating. No, he didn't defend me; no, he didn't even ask if it was true. It was assumed that because of my past, I was guilty. I had zero idea who these men were speaking about. I was on my best behavior at the gym and had no association with anyone from the gym, except the greeting from the trainer and the brief conversations with the regulars during my workouts. Apparently, someone had witnessed the interchanged between the guy behind the counter and me and reported it as dating to the Hatchet Man. I asked who my accuser was and was told that was confidential. Again, I was the one with the past and not to be trusted.

My dad immediately blamed me for his lack of promotion within the congregation. I was 100 percent innocent of the accusation, and no one cared.

I believe now that Dad was lost, no direction or identity without his titles, and no intimate relationship with his heavenly Father to fall back on. If he had one, I know he would have taught me how to have one too. Dad studied all their literature and was a great speaker as an elder. Once he wasn't an elder anymore, he seemed to forget who gave him those gifts, and it wasn't a man… God anoints and appoints, not the Hatchet Man or a visiting overseer.

During this time, another man was reinstated after being disfellowshipped for several years. He was being mentored by a few of the ministerial servants, and as such, he was invited to a lot of the same gatherings I was. He had his own business and house, and even though he wasn't a very kind or gracious individual, he was already considered a catch. The idea that he, too, had been disfellowshipped and, therefore, just as tarnished as me did cross my mind as well. I let it be known in our circle that I might be interested. But within a few weeks, he had many desperate single sisters flocking to him at the meetings. I heard rumor that these women were even preparing and bringing him meals to get his attention. The fact that marrying in the Lord is a requirement to be considered a loyal servant of God seems to tip the scales toward the brothers. It is typical to have one brother hotly pursued by several sisters, regardless of his personality, appearance, or disposition. So here I was, one of many, standing in line for my turn for this man's attention.

One evening, I was out for a drive with an old friend. She was the wife of one of that man's mentors. As I began stating my interest and why I would be a good mate for him, she interrupted me with "I know what you did to get disfellowshipped. I can't even look at you without thinking about it. I don't think you would be good for him." There it was, my spiritual red letter handed back to me to securely fasten back on my chest as if I had accidentally dropped it somewhere, and she was politely giving it back to me.

From that evening on, the brother kept his distance from me. For years, I wondered if she had told him the thing she couldn't stop thinking every time she looked at me? Did he think he was better than me, that my sin was worse than his?

Frankly, if that was who God wanted for me none of the gossip would've mattered. I thank God today, even though it was painful then. He spared me a life with a self-righteous, perfectionist brother.

I would like to say at any given time during this year-long trek back to God that I got it, that I finally understood that God was for me, not against me. I did not. I continued to throw myself into the spiritual boxing ring to be beaten with Bibles and literature by every member of the congregation who felt compelled to do so. I was taught that it all came from God...because they said it did.

There came a day, about a year after I was reinstated, that I gave up. I was tired of trying to get approval from the congregation and prove I wasn't bad. I knew I would have to move out of my parents' house if I decided to pursue anything not of their religion. I had begun to work full time in the basement of a large family-owned department store, and one of my coworkers had a room for rent for $100 a month. I told her I would love to, but because she wasn't a member of my religion, they wouldn't let me.

She reminded me I was now eighteen years old and, as such, free to make my own decisions and move out. I was a legal adult, and no one could stop me. She was so excited for me because I was a '90s woman, part of a generation of women that could be independent and make choices other women before me couldn't. An aha moment for sure. I decided to take the leap. I had my mom meet me for lunch the very next day and told her my plan. She was very supportive and said she understood. Within the week, I began preparing for the move.

At the same time, I started working out after hours with another guy from the gym. We flirted and joked, and I sincerely just wanted to date and be young. I knew that casual dating was a no-no, and dating a nonbeliever was grounds for another round of discipline from the elders. Knowing I would soon be out of my parents' house, I started spending more time at the gym and, thus, more time with him and away from the organization. My mom even met him when he came to pick me up for our first date right before I moved out.

The night before my exit, Mom panicked. I don't know; maybe she thought I would lose my nerve or change my mind and not go through with my new life. She must have realized I was packed and ready to go, and that's when she lost it, throwing her coffee cup across the living room in exasperation. She blurted out that I was ruining my life and would end up pregnant, alone, and destitute within a year. I really didn't see that coming; she had seemed so supportive up until that moment. Her outburst of fear only fueled my ambition to get out of their house.

The next day, as I prepared to leave my bedroom for the last time, my parents made it clear they would not be helping me move into my new home. This venture wasn't viewed by them as a typical exciting coming of age, my first apartment moment. Instead, it was called leaving the truth in which death would eventually result.

The lie that there is only one way to serve the Lord and only one organization that is clean in His eyes was deeply entrenched in me for decades and continues to be in my parents and the religious organization they belong to even as I write this. Any deviation from the endless rules they teach as Christian living is not just considered unclean but also as apostasy.

But that view is a portrait of the Pharisees and Sadducees, and Jesus clearly condemned those groups of men multiple times in the Bible.

"For Everyone who calls on the name of
the Lord will be saved." (Romans 10:13
NLT)

"He has shown you, O mortal, what is good. And what does the Lord require of you? To act justly and to love mercy and walk humbly with your God." (Micah 6:8 NIV)

The truth is, God doesn't limit Himself to speaking or moving within one organization or church that meticulously keeps score for Him. He loves us and desires a relationship, one on one, with each of us.

This was a pivotal, life-changing decision for me. I wish I could say this is when I opened my eyes and heart to God and walked with Him from that moment on. Instead, I met a new god, whom I would pursue with all my heart, mind, and strength for the twenty-two years after that.

CHAPTER 9

I'm Free, I'm Free…Now What?

Everything in my life changed overnight. That night, as I sat in my new home, I realized I didn't have to do anything anymore. I could make decisions based on what I thought was right or wrong. No more spending endless hours studying and going to meetings. No more confessing my every mistake to the elders. I wanted a fresh start. Living on my own, I decided I would find out who I was. I wanted my life to be different. I just didn't know what that would look like when every thought, feeling, and action had been dictated previously.

I wanted change, and boy did I get that

The new home was the opposite of the home I was accustomed to. The room I rented was in a flat on the second story of a building on the waterfront in a section of town called Old Town. I rented one of six rooms with a communal living room, bathroom, and kitchen. There were six of us living in the flat. Three of my roommates were male musicians in their thirties with the lifestyle of late nights and later mornings. One of the other roommates rented her room basically for storage. There were different stories as to where she was, although I don't think I ever actually met her. Then there was my coworker. She tried to balance her nine-to-five life at the department store with her boyfriend's musician lifestyle.

The history of the building in which the flat was located dates to the early 1900s, and our flat was rumored to have been a notorious brothel. The walls were covered with anything and everything that could be described as outrageous. I lived there for four months and still had not read or seen every item secured to the walls. I was shown which shelf in both the refrigerator and the cupboards would be mine. Along with the monthly rent for my room, I was now responsible to buy my own food, keep it separate from everyone else's, prepare it, and clean up after myself in a way that was respectful to five other individual standards.

My address wasn't the only thing that had changed. I now had endless hours of free time on my hands. I began filling my time at the gym, training for various bodybuilding and powerlifting contests. I split my time between work, working out, and pursuing the guy from the gym.

He has another story altogether.

He had just gotten out of the military and was working part-time at the gym for some cash while he waited to go fishing in Alaska. He made it very clear right from the start that he didn't want any attachments to anyone or anything because the trip would be treacherous, and he didn't want anyone trying to keep him from going and making a ton of money.

At first, we simply both had extra time, so we just hung out, mostly at the gym or in his bed. But soon, I began to hang on to every word he uttered and found ways to bring him up in all my conversations with anyone and everyone. I was enamored with his quick wit and our mutual obsession with the gym. But I also saw a kindred spirit in the way he rebelled against life by growing out his hair and putting on muscle weight because he didn't have the regulations of the military dictating his appearance anymore. I, too, felt that same rebelliousness being on my own for the first time.

The more I pushed for his attention, though, the more he pushed me away. I was obsessed with him. He became my new source of truth and direction. If he said hanging out together and having sex with no commitment was normal dating, I believed it. If he felt I was too clingy because I wanted to go on real dates and call him my boyfriend, I blamed myself for not knowing how to exist outside of my parents' home. Meanwhile, he was enjoying the undivided attention I had for every word he uttered as well as my enthusiasm for our physical relationship, all with no ties or boundaries.

The first party I ever attended was at that flat I lived in and was just a few weeks after I moved in. It was a birthday party for my coworker. Our birthdays are one day apart, and she graciously suggested we celebrate both birthdays that day. I was excited to be able to make the choice to be at a real party and so close to my own birthday; I was turning nineteen.

The day of the party felt so awkward. As we prepared for the festivities, we started drinking early. I wasn't accustomed to drinking and quickly became that obnoxious girl with a big mouth who doesn't remember much about anything the next day. It was an epic party, or so I was told by my not-boyfriend who came to the party that night.

The chasm between my coworker and I grew overnight. She went from big sister/confidant to avoiding me at home and work.

Within a week, she asked to take me to lunch. Because we hadn't been talking much, I naively thought this was a kind gesture to reconnect. I was wrong. At lunch, she explained that the other roommates were not comfortable with me in the house. There were a lot of grievances I had committed without even knowing it. For instance, I was not accustomed to coming and going freely and, therefore, had been notifying the roommates every time I came and went, and when I might be returning, which made these cool musicians feel like they were my parents. Not good. I had not been a good steward of the shelf system for food and had eaten someone else's bread and spilt my orange juice in the kitchen and had not cleaned it up properly as well. But the last straw had been the drunken yelling out of "It's my birthday too! I'm nineteen!" at the party the weekend prior—which, I, of course, couldn't even remember because I was drunk, and illegally so. She was the messenger and was sent to let me know I didn't fit here either. She knew of a mutual friend who was a single mom that needed a solid roommate to help with the rent. This, we decided, would be a better fit for me. We drove to her house later that day, and a new living arrangement was made.

That single move saved our friendship. She went from being my first roommate to being my mentor on how to be a '90s woman from then on.

In hindsight, I was much more at home in the suburbs with the picket fence and the family atmosphere. I had a small little room, but it had a lot of natural lighting and felt happy and peaceful. I soon fell into a comfortable routine—early rise, work out, work, work out again, go find the boy, back to bed, repeat. I didn't know who I was, but I had a feeling who he might want, and I strived to be that.

The relocation brought some unwelcome visitors too. Since I had left the religion without admitting to any wrongdoing, I wasn't disfellowshipped. This meant that people in the congregation could still talk to me.

Car groups of old friends would be out in the ministry and stop by randomly to check on me. At first this seemed really kind, and I appreciated it. But soon, I began to feel pursued in a way that felt like they were trying to catch me doing something wrong.

One time, they stopped by a house I was house-sitting. It just so happened that the boy had slept over, and his truck was parked out front. I tried to ignore the knocks at the door, but they didn't stop. I left the bedroom where he was still sleeping, closing the bedroom door behind me. I answered the door to my sister standing there very uncomfortably, saying, "Hi…uh…we were in the neighborhood, and…uh, we all wanted to see you." I glanced over her shoulder, and who was driving? The Hatchet Man.

I told her it wasn't a good time, and she looked over her shoulder at the van and said, "He's the one that wanted to stop. Just go say hi, and we'll leave, okay?" I obliged. The "saying hi" turned into an interrogation of questions. Was I alone? Who was with me? Was I dating? I deflected all his questions and said goodbye. Later, I called my sister and wanted to know "What the heck?" She told me she endured those questions while out in the ministry every time she was put in his group and that he was on the hunt for evidence to officially remove me from the congregation. She ended the call with "Please be careful!"

I was grasping at so many things, trying to fill the void the loss of religion had made. I was fighting depression constantly. I had been indoctrinated with the belief that without their religion, there was no God listening to me. I sought ways to fill the spiritual gap that left.

I competed in my first powerlifting meet that spring. On the drive home with my mom and my giant trophy, the pride and accomplishment were deflated as my mom asked, "Is this really what you gave up Jehovah for?" She couldn't understand any pursuit outside of the organization. She had never allowed herself that luxury.

A few months later, I competed in my first and last bodybuilding show. The high from the trip with my girlfriends combined with the performance on stage felt amazing to me. The cheering crowd, the music and lights, all of it made me feel accepted for the first time in my life. But that, too, was short-lived.

Within a week, I felt even lower than before. I was exhausted. I thought there was something physically wrong and wanted to go to the doctor, but I had no insurance. I called in sick from work and went to see my mom at the store she was working at. She convinced me to go to the clinic and have tests done to make sure I hadn't caught anything from my new lifestyle. Although I laughed it off, denying I was doing anything I could catch a disease from, I started to become worried that she could be right. From her store, I went straight to the clinic just to be safe. Of course, all my tests came back clean. The kind nurse practitioner suggested the yo-yo diet I had been on the past few months combined with the birth control pills I started taking were probably to blame and sent me off to the pharmacy for a good multivitamin.

The next day, I went to work and was called up to Human Resources. I hung up the phone in anticipation as I had never been up to those offices before. I was naïve enough to think I had been doing such a good job that I was being called into the executive offices for a promotion of some sort. But instead, it was revealed to me that my manager had been having lunch out and about the previous day and had seen me go into my mom's store. Although there were no previous violations or history of broken store polices, I was fired on the spot for calling off without being sick. Once again, I was being punished for something I didn't do. Of course, I protested and offered to provide proof that I had gone to the doctor. I not so proudly retrieved my evidence from the clinic, proving I had been treated, but Human Resources didn't back down.

Today, that sort of treatment by a business wouldn't be tolerated. There are laws that protect you when you are ill. But that was the '90s, and it was a small, family-owned business. The family was a powerful name in the community; anything they did was accepted, no questions asked.

In the meantime, my gym crush had opted out of the treacherous trip to Alaska and decided to stay put and get a job at the local mill. But he still didn't want to label whatever it was that we were doing, so he demanded I not refer to him as my boyfriend. As much as I tried to prove how good I could be for him and to him, he wanted an open relationship with no commitments.

So here I was, jobless, with no definable relationship and no real connection to family. What a failure.

I applied at Montgomery Ward the next day and got hired the same day. It was only then that I felt I could tell my roommate that I had lost my job and found a new one. I called her and told her we needed to talk when she got off work. We lived in such a small town, I feared someone would tell her I had lost my job before I could tell her I was gainfully employed and still dependable. When she came home from work that night, she told me she needed to talk to me as well. She had decided to move in with her boyfriend and was giving notice on the house we shared.

What was I going to do now? I had not even been out of my parents' house for eight months and had already lost not one but two places to live. Had they all been right? Was I just not acceptable anywhere in the world, inside or outside of their religion?!

That night, when I was at my lowest, I suggested to my nonboyfriend that we get our own place and move in together. He thought about it for a few days but ultimately agreed to it. Finally! We would move in together, keeping it a secret from my family, of course, but making us a couple to the rest of the world. He conceded that we would agree to be exclusive, but "I'm never going to marry you, no matter what. I'm never getting married again." He had been married briefly before we met and had not recovered from the pain of that abrupt ending. I didn't care at that moment about the backhanded rejection he had just laid on me; I was just excited to have a boyfriend.

Within a month of moving in, my sisters had both come to visit, and it became obvious that those weren't my size 11 boots in the closet. My mom and dad decided the game of hide-and-seek had gone on long enough, and a rescue mission was put into play. I was to pack all my belongings and go live with my uncle in Redding, get myself back to the meetings, and back in good standing with the congregation; *or* they would tell the elders there in Eureka at which time the Hatchet Man would be given free rein to wield his mighty weapon on me one more time.

When my boyfriend came home from the gym that day, I told him that my mom had visited and the ultimatum that I was given. He was genuinely sad and didn't want me to leave. He said he had fallen in love with me and could possibly see us having a future together. I was sick. I had waited so long for those small crumbs, but if I didn't leave, I would be forced to live an outcast's life again. Up until then, I was living a debauched life but not going to meetings, so therefore, no action was being taken against me by my former church. Kind of like a religious "don't ask, don't tell." But now, with my family aware I was living in sin, they had to either rescue me from it or turn me into the elders. If they didn't, they would be seen as accomplices and would be subject to the Hatchet Man's judgment themselves.

So I packed up again, but this time, it felt wrong. My sister, her husband, and my mom picked me up and loaded my bags into our cars to move me. Our three cars felt like a funeral procession as we left my apartment. We stopped for pizza on the way out of town. It was at that table that I made another huge decision. I told them I couldn't go. Moving to Redding, leaving the man that I had finally heard "I love you" from, going back to the religion, all of it. My stomach turned, and my heart pounded as I told them to take me back to my apartment. I couldn't leave my new life even if that meant I would have to face dire consequences for it.

I thought my boyfriend would be happy that I had chosen to stay, but that is far from how he felt. He was hurt by the fact that I could desert him so easily. He was angry that I had put him on an emotional roller coaster. He didn't even want to see me. He spent the next few days teetering between ignoring my presence and sneering that "this is exactly why he never wanted a girlfriend."

As if that wasn't unpleasant enough, the Hatchet Man had received the news of my living arrangement and called to let me know he and another elder would be coming to talk to me within the week. He made it sound as if they wanted to help me come back to Jehovah. The night they arrived, I cleaned the house and made muffins and coffee. I don't know what I was thinking with that gesture; clearly, I was in denial about how this visit would end.

Within five minutes of their arrival, he turned to me and said, "Enough small talk. Are you living with a man here? Are you intimate?"

I was so shocked I responded yes and yes.

He gathered up his things and said, "Well, we will be disfellowshipping you then. You know that, right?" He went on a five-minute rant about how he had known I was unclean and shouldn't ever have been reinstated. I nodded, unable to even speak. It was the road I had taken; this was the consequence. As they got up to leave the other elder, a very close family friend, tried to soften the encounter by being encouraging, telling me to take care of myself and know that I'm loved.

Then the Hatchet Man swung open the door and said, "Do yourself a favor and use birth control. You don't want to get pregnant again." He turned to the other man with him and said, "Let's go. This is making my stomach turn." Both turned on their heels, left my home, and took God with them.

The announcement to the congregation happened a week later. Although expulsion from their organization requires a body of three elders, I found out later they got around this policy by simply writing "refused to meet" in my file. So I was disfellowshipped once again, removed from their religion and, in effect, from God himself.

That was the last time I ever saw or spoke to the Hatchet Man. I hear he is still in that organization, spreading the lie that God is a merciless god, one of judgment and punishment and loves only those with perfect obedience to every law within that organization. He has boldly used the Bible to excuse the reckless use of his man-given power, lopping off the spiritual heads of young and old. To this day, most of my childhood friends do not believe there is a good, loving God because of the way he used his hatchet to injure their soul as if he knows what only God does.

The lie that I believed then was that when you step out of line, you should be chased down and removed from others, so as not to contaminate God's pure people. I truly believed that was from God himself.

The truth is that Jesus spoke at length on those that stray or even walk away and how God always chases down the lost to bring them back into His fold. The story of the lost sheep and prodigal son are great examples Christ gave of how our God truly feels about us.

> "Suppose one of you has a hundred sheep and loses one of them. Doesn't he leave the ninety-nine in the open country and go after the lost sheep until he finds it? I tell you that in the same way there will be more rejoicing in heaven over one sinner who repents than over the ninety-nine righteous persons who do not need to repent." (Luke 15:4, 7 NIV)

I was an adult, answering only to myself now. I had the ability to be free, and yet I wasn't. I couldn't allow myself that. I was still believing all their lies that I wasn't worthy of love or approval from anyone, especially not from God.

But now I would replace listening and chasing after the approval of that group of men to panting and longing for one man.

CHAPTER 10

Looking for Love in All the Wrong Faces

Within a few weeks, all the drama seemed to settle. My boyfriend and I were falling into a nice routine of working out, work, and sleep. Once the announcement was made to the congregation that I was disfellowshipped again, there were no more surprise visits or phone calls.

It was at this phase in my life that I had the ability to make choices to align myself with my created purpose. Unfortunately, without that religion, I believed I did not have God's favor, let alone His love. I began to pursue any and every way to be loved in lieu of that.

My boyfriend's mom was a huge part of his life and, soon, mine too. She is an excellent cook and would make easy but delicious meals, and we came over to hang out often. I saw the way he looked to her for advice or opinions and respected her. I began to see her the same way he did. She and I became very good friends. Together we would craft, Christmas shop, and just talk and laugh. She is one of the most energetic and ingenious people I've ever known. In her, I saw a skill set that I had never seen in anyone, man or woman. She tore apart and redid her decking multiple times, roofed both her homes ("It's just like quilting," she would say), painted her houses inside and out, and did all the yardwork, all while caring for her husband who was older and had a long-term illness. She was not happy unless she had a project.

She is a super woman; I admire her immensely.

In the absence of both the organization and my own mom, she became my role model, the person I wanted to be like, the person I wanted to be liked by. At first, it was because I began to believe that if I was more like her, he would love me like he loved her. But that evolved into a much deeper bond. I had never been in a functional family with loyalty and respect just because you were blood-related like theirs is. In my world, there were always conditions, unattainable goals, and rules to uphold to have that kind of love. I longed to have their love. To be a part of that kind of love.

He and I were on again, off again many times over the next few years, but I always said his mom was one of the reasons I kept coming back. I loved her as much as I loved him.

My employer at that time was Montgomery Ward, and that was going well. I was happy with my $5.25 an hour, a decent amount at the time for a girl with no education or formal training. I was good at my job and felt a sense of camaraderie in the department-store world. To supplement my income, I also taught my own fitness classes at the gym three mornings a week as well as being a substitute for other time slots as needed. I was comfortable.

One afternoon at a luncheon to honor performers, another attendee slipped a business card in my hand and told me to go talk to the manager. She said she had seen my work ethic and felt strongly I could have a successful career in jewelry. After some prodding from my Wards colleague, I called the man on the business card. We scheduled an interview for later that week.

On the day of the interview, after I finished teaching one of my classes, I reluctantly went in to meet the manager. The interview was done by both the manager and the visiting district manager. The district manager (DM) was dressed in an expensive suit and was a smooth talker, almost slick. When he shook my hand, he said with an arrogant smirk, "Oh, relax, you will do fine."

Puzzled, I said, "I am relaxed."

To which he laughingly said, "Then why are your hands hot?"

And I responded, "I'm a part-time fitness instructor, and I just finishing teaching a class." I was put off immediately by his arrogance. But the interview went well, and I was offered the job, making $6 an hour, plus bonuses. I was ecstatic.

Now I think it is here I must say this: I have learned in my fifty-two years that when you get a bad feeling in your gut with a first impression, you should hang onto that. Sometimes, God is putting that feeling in your heart. Discernment is like a big, giant internal warning. Listen!

So at twenty years old, I began working for the jewelry business. The same business I have been in for thirty-two years.

The work was exciting, and I quickly found I was good at it. The second month into my new job, I was the number one salesperson in the store. For the first time in my life, I felt celebrated somewhere for what I brought to the table. My coworkers were like family, and the customers appreciated my service and follow-up. I was genuinely beginning to develop confidence in myself, my abilities, and my skills.

I also caught the eye of the DM. I would call him for discounts or to authorize a transaction, and he would tell me to call him back once I made the sale. After the guest paid and left, I would call him on his car phone (this was the '90s; car phones were very impressive). He told me how amazing I was; the potential he knew was there from the beginning. Flattery, flowery, yet empty words. I was so starved emotionally and mentally of any validation that even the smallest tidbit from someone in power, even though he was manipulating me, was a full meal that would fill me up for days. I would go home from work after a successful sales day, grinning from ear to ear, only to be met by my boyfriend who would inform me he was going out with his friends, and I wasn't invited. I tried pretending it didn't hurt me, smiling and agreeing to be right there waiting for him. Those nights were always sleepless until he stumbled home in the wee hours of the morning, reeking of alcohol and passing out, unable to remember much the next day. Of course, I shared these heartbreaks with a very sympathetic DM on our next phone call.

We had big diamond events in our store, and it was customary for the DM to come to those shows and, if successful, take everyone out for drinks afterward. It was after one of these shows that an inappropriate relationship was born. We went to the bar at his hotel as a group. I had a great show, and the accolades and compliments were more intoxicating than the cocktails. After everyone left, the DM walked me to my car, making it very clear he didn't want me to leave. I reminded him that he was married, and I had a boyfriend. He stated that my boyfriend had probably cheated on me when he went out with the boys. "Why bring the sand to the beach?" he said. As for his wife, he claimed they were separated.

That was the first time I kissed him. But it was only the beginning.

After that encounter, for the next two years, every time he visited, if my boyfriend and I were broken up (which happened often in the four years we dated), he and I would meet at his hotel bar and inevitably end up in his room. The physical relationship was only consummated a handful of times over those two years. The addiction to his words and praise were year-round. It was a vicious cycle of highs of his validation, followed by lows of him ignoring me for weeks at a time. Feeling the strength from this man's affections would help me stand up for myself in other areas of life, but the second he disappeared, I would crawl back to a boyfriend who never really wanted a relationship, let alone a committed one. I would start trying to earn my boyfriend's affections again, literally selling him on the idea of me as his girlfriend.

I was promoted to assistant manager within a year, but after that, there were no opportunities presented to me for several years. There were many excuses given. I was told it was because I was young and inexperienced. I was great in the small town, but how good would I really be in a bigger, different city? In fact, every vice president that came through town with him quickly put me off, telling me I was just a good salesgirl, nice on the eyes, but not promotable. Many times, in those exact words.

I was desperately searching for confirmation that I was accepted somewhere by someone. When I sold well, I bonussed well. When I was bonused well, I had enough money to pay my bills comfortably and buy nice things for my boyfriend and me. When I bought nice things for him, he was interested again; he wanted me around more. During the up months, I'm sure I also exuded a certain amount of confidence, which is always more attractive. If he grew bored of me and went out with the guys and ignored me? I would seek my approval and love at work.

A vicious cycle.

During this time, there were moments of acceptance and then rejection from my family as well.

One Christmas, I was celebrating the holidays with my boyfriend and his family when my sister called. She had given birth and wanted me to meet my new niece. I dropped everything and rushed to the hospital. As I held this little bundle of absolute joy, my heart connected to hers. At that moment, I began to long for my family. I wanted to be able to be a part of her life. In the months and years that followed, I would find little dresses and bring them to their home, looking for just a glance at her, a connection. But as soon as my family realized that I was not coming back to the religion, I was asked to quit showing up and interrupting their lives with false hope of my return to the religion.

This routine of reaching, hoping, and ultimately rejection went on for several years before I wanted more for my life. This naively led to me giving my boyfriend an ultimatum; marry me, or I would leave for good. I thought marriage would give me a permanent bond with someone. Although he genuinely cared for me, he had his own wounds he was hiding, protecting his heart. He stalled the answer for several weeks but ultimately told me to go because he was never going to marry me.

At this point, work was now having its struggles. I had left a mall employee's ring in the ring clinic (jewelry cleaner) and let her go back to work while they soaked. This was a customary procedure at the time. The store manager, in a rush to get back to his desk, took in an uncounted number of pieces from another group of guests, threw them into the cleaner, and then proceeded to give them back all their pieces as well as the mall employee's rings. He sat back at his desk, unaware of what he had just done.

As soon as the mistake was discovered, there were a lot of consequences. The mall employee came back to pick up her rings, only to discover the ring clinic was turned off and empty. Loss prevention was called, and an investigation ensued. We immediately began procedures to replace the guest's ring, but she was so distraught by the loss that no substitute was good enough. Her marriage was struggling, and she blamed me because I had lost the item that represented her marriage. Giving her ring to someone else, she felt, was causing her marriage to fail. My manager took no responsibility and told the investigator that we don't let guests leave the store while we clean their pieces (we discovered it was against company policy by the time he was interviewed), and that I had single-handedly broken company policy of my own accord. After a brief investigation, the investigator decided we were equally at fault, wrote us both up, and had us sign a document stating that we would pay the company back with a weekly payroll deduction for the cost of the ring.

I felt like such a failure again. I had no boyfriend. I had lost the respect of that customer. I had left my company exposed to liability, and as a result, they had turned their back on me. I had been abandoned by management and was left with a substantial financial burden ($3,000, the cost to replace her ring).

Believe it or not, it was at this point that I was offered my first relocation, a lateral move that was presented to me by the DM as a promotion. So within two weeks with nothing to lose, I left my small town, moving four hours away to the city of Santa Rosa. I was propelled by my need to feel accepted and approved of, and that was no longer in the small town of Eureka. The DM convinced me this move could show upper management that I had what it took to work in any environment and that I was willing to make sacrifices for the company. He told me the promotion to store manager would follow. The move was financially wrong for me, but with no mom or dad to advise me, I made the decision to go anyway.

The morning after my move, my boyfriend called. He said he had gone to my apartment, and it was empty. It shook him. He didn't want to lose me; he wanted to marry me. With my heart leaping out of my chest, I reminded him how strongly he opposed marriage and suggested he think about it for a few days. When he called me a few days later, his proposal was "Even though you are not a 'ten,' maybe a 'ten' is not coming around for me. Maybe you are the best I'm gonna get." A little insulted, I hesitated and told him the man I marry should think I am a ten. Flustered, he said that didn't come out right, and that isn't what he meant and insisted I come back to Eureka and marry him. He was so persuasive, and my heart wanted his love so badly. I got off the phone, engaged.

The day came for the same DM to come to my new store to visit. By this time, as this new location was his home store, I had discovered that he had multiple women just like me in several of his assigned stores. A girl at every port was what I was told by the office manager at this store that fielded his not-so-appropriate mail and phone calls. Not only was I struggling financially from the move without any real pay increase, but I also had a new biweekly payroll deduction to loss prevention for the ultrasonic incident. My infatuation with the DM was now completely gone. Walking to our cars at the end of his store visit, he said he just remembered he had the training monitor still with him and asked if he could leave it at my apartment so it would be there in the event our store needed it. The store was closed, the alarm set, and everyone but the two of us had left the parking lot. He said it was valuable, so he didn't want me to leave it in my trunk where it could get stolen. All lies intended to persuade me to lead him to my apartment. Reluctant, I told him yes and gave him my address. In hindsight, I could've had him put the equipment in my trunk and bid him a good night. It wasn't as heavy as he said it was, so I could've brought it into my apartment that night and back into my car to work the next day.

But I didn't. I guess I still sought his approval, and like a child, a small part of me wanted his opinion of my new apartment. I was home less than five minutes before there was a knock at my door. Once inside my apartment, he was all over me. I told him I was engaged, and this was not going to happen anymore. He tried to convince me with the smoothest of words and his best sales skills to rethink that decision. When that didn't work, he resorted to berating me. I was stupid for marrying this guy who clearly cheats on me and other hypocritical hurtful words. But ultimately, he left my home with the parting words "I don't know if I would've promoted you here if I knew this is how it would be." He never gave me any more positive feedback or commendations after that. Even though I was one of the top performers in the entire region, I was also not even recommended for any promotions by him after that.

I began taking the long drive, 240 miles each way, weekly to spend time with my new fiancé. The thrill of being engaged was soon deflated, though, when he started denying to our friends that he had proposed. First, he told me that he didn't want a big wedding. Then he demanded we keep the engagement a secret; he didn't want anyone to know we were engaged. I wanted to shout it from the rooftops: I was getting married to the man I had chased for four years! But ultimately, there was that part of me that felt unworthy of real acceptance, so hiding and secrets were comfortable; it had been the kind of love I had received my whole life.

Within six months, I requested a transfer back to Eureka and resumed the assistant manager role in my old store.

Three months later, we were married at a very small ceremony in Reno, Nevada. On the long drive to our wedding venue, he nervously looked at me and said, "I didn't bring my social security card. If we can't get married without it, we will tell everyone we got married and leave it at that, okay?" My stomach dropped. I began to pray to a God I didn't think even heard me to please make this wedding happen. I was desperate. The idea that he would be okay pretending to be married made me feel rejected once again, unwanted and undeserving of a loving commitment.

But the wedding was in the state of Nevada, and no documentation was necessary. We went into the courthouse and came out ten minutes later with our license.

We were married on May 2, 1994. There was a total of six of us present—my husband-to-be and me; my mother-in-law, who was my matron of honor; my father-in-law, who walked me down the aisle; my brother-in-law, who was the best man; and my sister-in-law, who took the pictures. No other guests and no other family. It didn't matter how many people were missing that day. I felt so loved and accepted that day that nothing else mattered.

The lie I believed and lived for so many years is that love could be earned from people, places, and even things.

I believed I could feel truly loved and fulfilled by things of this earth. At the same time, I believed it could all be taken away if I didn't comply with any superficial demands or whims of those around me.

The truth is that love—real, original love—comes from above and never leaves. He made us exactly the way we are supposed to be, and He's happy we exist just the way He created us. No chasing after His love; in fact, He chases after us!

> "Give thanks to the God of gods. His faithful love endures forever." (Psalm 136:2 NLT)

> "I have loved you, my people, with an everlasting love. With unfailing love I have drawn you to myself." (Jeremiah 31:3 NLT)

We all have regrets. Mine is spending so much of my life looking for love where it can only temporarily be found and so easily lost. I was twenty-three years old and thought I had finally found real love and, in turn, my happily ever after. I was wrong.

CHAPTER 11

I Can, I Will...I Do

The years of effort I had spent proving I was worth marrying did not end once we were married.

As soon as we drove home from our honeymoon, we were met with unforeseen bills that caused stress. Seeing my husband so upset made me feel obligated to fix it. I stepped up by teaching more classes at the gym as well as putting us on a loose budget to get our finances together. Everything I did from that moment on was very calculated. Finding ways to impress, comfort, satisfy, or in any way please my then husband became my focus. By this time, he was hunting, fishing, and camping every spare moment he got. If I wanted to spend time with him, I needed to pursue the same hobbies. I took a hunter's safety course to get my hunting license to be able to go hunting with him August through October. I spent many uncomfortable nights out in the brush in a tent with only a set of shrubs as a bathroom. We sat around the campfire in the evenings drinking beer with his childhood hunting buddy that would utter funny stories at first, followed by contempt toward me for being there as he stumbled to his tent and passed out at the end of the night. I tried to not let that bother me. I was happy just to be invited to the party. But that is, if I was invited. Many times, I wasn't. I found myself panting after him. Always trying to have the same opinions and mindset that he had. I would do and be anything he wanted if it meant being near him. But he worked swing shift, leaving me with a lot of time alone to think and, subsequently, feel loneliness.

I had thought being his wife would fulfill me, that I would feel loved and content. Of course, I wanted him to fill a void only God can, which was unrealistic. Instead, the emptiness was still hanging heavily over me. It was then that I began searching for something or someone to make me feel whole.

In the beginning, working long hours late into the evening and then dinners with friends on the nights I didn't work were enough. But soon, my eyes began to wander. I would scan the bar at the restaurant and fantasize that someone there would see me and want me. Surely then, I would feel valued, right?

It was at one of those dinners that I met a friend of a friend. A male friend. I do not recall how it all began, who called whose workplace first, but we soon started talking on the phone. He came to my work for lunch, and a few times, I came over to his home. We met up and went on drives, which typically ended with kissing. On one of those drives, we stopped to see his parents. They were lovely, and I could tell they really adored him. It made me feel an odd sadness, and for the first time, I felt guilty about the relationship. I guess, because the relationship hadn't progressed sexually, I easily rationalized that what I was engaging in was okay. But after that moment at his parents', I realized it absolutely wasn't. In fact, it scared me. I knew then that I had become a cheater.

How could I have walked down this dangerous path? My husband was not a jealous man, far from it, but I was possessive and jealous. How would I feel if the roles were flipped and he was spending time with someone else, justifying it as no big deal because they didn't consummate it?

Scared, I began to believe that without the religion I was raised with, I would be an immoral, adulterous wife within the first year of my marriage if I didn't return to the church.

Also, I longed for my family, friends, and church. Now that I was married, I could be considered clean in their eyes and be reinstated.

Abruptly, I stopped the relationship and went back to the meetings before I ruined my marriage.

The challenges of this new pursuit came soon after.

To my new husband who was now used to being my focus and influencing most of my decisions, going back to that religion would not be something he would support. I knew this and went to the meetings behind his back. A double life once again.

The first few months were easy as my husband left for work at two and wasn't back until almost midnight. I could go to Tuesday and Thursday night meetings undetected. But as it got closer to applying for reinstatement, there were certain changes that needed to be made if I was to be accepted back into that organization. Not excessively drinking was easy enough, and since he really wasn't a gift giver, Christmas and birthdays really were a nonissue. But there was an election coming up. We had a tradition of sitting in bed the night before voting to go over how I would vote to further our political party. It was at this point that I had to tell him I'm no longer voting as I had begun going back to the meetings and trying to get back into the church. He was furious! In hindsight, I can see what a huge bait and switch I had done to him. He had married someone that had no family attachment and religion was a nonissue, and now within the first year, that was all about to change, and not in a good way in his eyes. After all, as a rule, he didn't like surprises or change.

He didn't speak to me for a few days after that. I called my parents to report the latest developments, and they were encouraging. I was taking a stand for Jehovah, my mom said; there would be trials and persecution. Mom encouraged me to continue to reveal only as much as necessary to him. She told me to try to be the best wife, not to talk back, and eventually, I would "win him without a word" (1 Peter 1:1, 2, their version).

That was not the only secret I was keeping, however, and I think he had his suspicions that there were more secrets being hidden from him.

A few weeks later, I walked into the kitchen to discover the contents of the cardboard box that I kept our bills and credit card statements in spread out on the kitchen table. There was a look of complete despair on my husband's face. Unbeknownst to him, I had accumulated thousands of dollars in debt. It had started with the move to Santa Rosa, then there was the planning and paying for a wedding with no parental support. But to be honest, it had continued as I bought gifts and took him and others out for meals, trying to prove I was financially independent. And as I was trying to fill the empty void, I had begun compulsively shopping as well. The facade that I was taking care of us, that we were debt-free, came crashing down with every bill he took out of that box.

In that instant, he was blinded with hurt and anger. We all have wounds and scars from our past, and this kind of financial betrayal was one of his. He didn't want to hear any more lies from me. He told me to get out of his house and never come back. Divorce? No, he was getting an annulment as I had deceived him from the beginning. The marriage was a lie, he said, and he wanted no record of his horrible mistake.

Since I was going to the meetings and trying to get reinstated, my mom and dad were trying to be there for me. Nonetheless, it was humiliating to call my parents and ask if I could move back in. They agreed that since I was trying to do what's right in the church's eyes, I could come there. Sobbing, I packed my clothes, my toiletries, and of course, my cardboard box of bills and left.

Shame and guilt were once again my companions.

Since I was still disfellowshipped, I had to spend much of my time in my room when I wasn't at work. The light in my day would be when my sister's now three-year-old daughter would sneak into my room to talk to me. On occasion, she would crawl in bed with me for a nap. I napped a lot during my stay there; depression had begun to envelope me. She filled my heart with so much love and joy during such a dark time. Although I daily wondered how my husband could throw me away so easily without even a discussion, somehow, that little girl kept me from drowning in my own tears, knowing there was someone that did want my love and attention.

Funny sidenote, since I was still disfellowshipped, no one was supposed to talk to me when I attended the weekly meetings. The routine of slipping in and then out of the meetings as unnoticed as possible was important to show my repentance. But once, as I was slipping quietly into the back row of the hall, that little cutie spotted me just as the meeting was about to start, and the room was dead silent. She excitedly pointed and called out, "Judy!" As her parents tried to act like they had no idea who she was talking about, she persisted, pointing in my direction with exasperation, "Yoook, Mom, it's Judy... But it's Judy, Dad, yoooook." She was so adorable. Now the gig was up; the whole congregation knew she was acquainted with me. She was as enamored by me as I was with her. For the first time, people smiled and chuckled and let us have that moment.

My then husband eventually called me at work. He was angry and accusatory at first, but once he realized he couldn't beat a dead horse anymore, he asked calmly, "Well, if we stay together, how are you going to pay these off?" That was a good question, but I absolutely knew I was up to the challenge to pay all my debt off and earn his love and trust back. We met later in the week, and I was given the opportunity to lay my plan out for him—how I would fix this. At this point, we also decided that the "no kids" statute I had agreed to for us to be married could be lifted as well, and we would revisit the idea of having a family once the bills were paid. We decided to give our marriage another chance.

The Hatchet Man had left the congregation. He had taken his family and run away from some financial issues to some unknown area on the East Coast. There was a new group of elders, younger and unjaded by their power who arranged the meeting with me to discuss repentance and reinstatement. It was at this meeting with the new elders that I was asked why I had "refused to meet" with the elders when I was disfellowshipped years prior. Surprised at this revelation, I told them of the visit to my home a few years prior and that I was told the two would be disfellow-shipping me. I had no knowledge that another meeting was required or that I had declined it. The new elders looked at each other with a knowing smile. In the absence of the Hatchet Man, I was reinstated quickly, and once again, within the seconds it takes to read the letter, the world is somehow righted, giving me full access to my family and friends.

Life was good.

Armed with a goal, I started paying everything off. With the bonuses I made selling jewelry, I paid off credit cards first then started on my car. When my car was paid off, I started on his truck. With every payment in full receipt I presented, trust was restored. When the novelty of that wore off, I knew I needed to do something grand to hold my husband's attention. It was then that I met with a loan officer and a contractor. I came home and unveiled how easily we could have our first home built. He was happy, so I was happy. This became our marital cycle. Any confidence I had was directly related to the money I made, attaching my self-worth to the company I worked for that gave me the opportunity to make that money. Honestly, even to this day, I sometimes struggle with how I see my value when I am not selling, achieving, or earning a lot.

The lie I believed was my value was in what I did on a daily basis, what I brought to the table of others and God every day.

The truth is that we are created through no doing of our own, and nothing can separate us from that love—nothing. Our value is in our having been created perfectly to do the will of God.

> "But, when God our Savior revealed his kindness and love, he saved us, not because of the righteous things we had done, but because of his mercy. He washed away our sins, giving us a new birth and life through the Holy Spirit." (Titus 3:4, 5 NLT)

> "For I am convinced that neither death nor life, neither angels nor demons, neither the present nor the future, nor any powers, neither height nor depth, nor anything else in all creation, will be able to separate us from the love of God that is in Christ Jesus our Lord." (Romans 8:38, 39 NIV)

But to be a part of the religious organization took total devotion to their practices. There were meetings, service, and study that needed to be done now as well as being submissive to my unbelieving mate. Could I balance them all and keep them both satisfied with me? Would one or both turn on me if I didn't?

I would almost die trying.

CHAPTER 12

I Think I Can, I Think I Can…until I Can't

The chunk of lies I was indoctrinated with up to this point shaped every decision, action, and goal. I believed that if I gave my best—my all, if you will—to both my husband and the religion, I would have their love and maybe even God's too. I told myself repeatedly that this was necessary, required, and nonnegotiable.

When we moved into our new home, I decided it was time to also change congregations. In this religion, you are assigned a congregation based on where your home is located. The new home was in a different city and, therefore, a different territory, a new congregation. It was not easy. I had always gone to the meetings with my parents, had basically the same lifelong circle of friends. Here I was in a new congregation with no friends or family. I went to the meetings completely alone. There were a few families that I knew of from growing up and going to assemblies and conventions together. I tried to connect with them.

One of my favorite things to do is share and give. I also love to go bargain shopping. About once a year, when my closet and dresser drawers become full, I go through and purge. I had told one of the women at church I was getting to know that I had purged and asked if she was interested in the results, two large trash bags full of clothes. She was a single mom with three young kids and excitedly accepted the offer. My husband was working that night, so she followed me home from the meeting. By the time we got to my house, all three of her littles were sound asleep in the car (meetings went until 9:15 p.m., way past a child's bedtime), so I went in and retrieved the bags while she waited with her car running in the driveway. When I returned, we started talking, which we did for a good thirty minutes. That night, I went to bed with a smile on my face, so happy to have made a connection in my new congregation.

The smile was short-lived.

The next day, my husband called me at work, clearly set off. He wanted to know who was at our home the night before and why. I went into panic mode as I often did when he was unhappy. He was a very private person and didn't like anyone, especially someone that he didn't know, in his home. After a few minutes of frantically explaining, I realized I had done nothing wrong and stopped myself from groveling. I asked why he was so mad, at which point he informed me that my new friend's car had leaked oil all over his new driveway. This was unacceptable! He demanded that I fix this by cleaning it up after I got off work that night (which was 9:30 p.m.). I remember being so afraid that if I couldn't get the stain off the driveway, it would be the last straw, the thing that finally drove him away. The fear of him being upset always led me to worry he would leave. I worried so much about this for the rest of my shift that I couldn't concentrate on my job. So on my way home, I stopped at a convenience store that was still open to get whatever scrub brushes and degreaser they had.

I was in the driveway scrubbing the oil (which ended up being the size of a softball) with a little plastic brush, bawling my eyes out when the very kind neighbor next door came over. He had watched me long enough to know what I was doing and offered me something better to clean the driveway. I must've been a sight. A young woman in the dark, in her dress clothes and jewelry, sobbing and scrubbing the cement outside her home. But much to my relief, his product worked perfectly. Catastrophe avoided.

In the spring of 1998, my boss, who was from the Sacramento area, wanted to move home. He was a single man with no friends or family in town, and he wasn't happy there. Eureka was not an easy place to recruit new managers, so there he grumpily sat for months waiting for the corporation to find his replacement. July came, and he made a phone call to our boss giving two weeks' notice if she didn't transfer him immediately. I had given up the idea of moving up in the company, but something about this new DM had given me the ambition to reach out to her for a future in management. She had taken an interest in not only my skills but in me as a person as well. She was a breath of fresh air with her Miss America personality and polite political correctness in a sea of male-dominated upper management.

On a whim, I called her and told her I was interested in taking his vacated position. After years of feeling blackballed for the relationship with my previous DM, I held little optimism that I would even be considered as a suitable replacement, let alone be given the promotion. I knew my work ethic and performance merited consideration, but I had been rejected for my imperfections so many times already that I wasn't hopeful I would be rewarded with this new position. To my surprise, she was excited at my interest. By August, I was the new store manager!

She was one of the best mentors I have ever had. She taught me everything I didn't know and then taught me to train others to pay it forward. She changed my work trajectory from having a job to having a career. I consider her to be one of the best humans working for that corporation, even to this day.

But I now had a third party to please to feel accepted and approved—a husband, a religion, and a large corporation.

To give you more insight into what this looked like, allow me to give the details of each party and their demands:

The Husband

He was a complicated and very private man with his own wounds and baggage, as we all have. Remember, he didn't really want a wife to begin with, and the idea that I had gone back to the very religion he had seen hurt me for years was disturbing to him. It had, in his opinion, sucked me back in. Although he did love me in his own way, he was suspicious and leery of me; my personality was outgoing and an open book to all, and he was introverted and private. I now was part of a religion that was considered a cult, and he was not going to let them get him too. I was very impulsive, optimistic, and sometimes naive about life and the religion; and he was reserved spiritually, outspoken politically, and pessimistic about my beliefs. We were quite an unmatched set. Instead of embracing our uniqueness, we both tried to change each other.

Let me stop at this fact: Knowing he didn't want to get married or be married did something to me psychologically. I was manipulated by my own mind to do and give and be whatever he needed so that he wouldn't leave me. I truly believed I was nothing worth keeping if I wasn't doing something of value. Years later, when I was the one that destroyed the marriage with my infidelity and had left, I told him after years of feeling like I was never enough for him, I broke and just couldn't do/give/be anymore. His response? "Julie, I would never have left you, it was never on my mind." My mind was blown.

But the biggest sacrifice I made to keep his favor was children, or shall I say, not having any. I had wanted children for as long as I could remember, fueled to some degree by my fatal decision as a teen. As friends of ours would start their families, I would bring up the subject of us starting ours, at which point he would always shut me down with an angry "Not this again!" If we spent time with his little nieces and I mentioned we needed to decide sooner rather than later about kids because we were getting older, he would say, "We already decided. We aren't having them." And if none of those responses shut me down, if I had the audacity to continue to pursue the matter, the response of "You can have them if you want...with someone else" always worked. It always scared me enough to leave the subject alone for a while. I didn't want to rock the boat and find myself thrown overboard by the captain of the ship.

When I turned to my parents for comfort and direction, I was told I shouldn't want a child anyway. My husband was an unbeliever, and the child would be raised conflicted and would be used as a tool of the devil to try to divide me from God. Not to mention the fact that we were living in the last days and then the scripture would be quoted in Matthew 24:19 (their version), "Woe to the pregnant women and those nursing a baby in those days."

The Religion

I was indoctrinated from infancy that this was the only true religion, the truth, as they referred to it as. All members are expected to view this organization and the men running it as Jehovah's organization. Not only were there three meetings a week that were considered mandatory, but they also had to be prepared for and every effort made to participate by raising your hand and commenting on the material in a deep enough way that your preparation was obvious but not so deep as to take any liberties with their printed page. There is no margin for free thinking within this organization; that is apostate. The conductor of each meeting had the liberty to pick and choose whose hand he would see and whose he would claim later he didn't see, based on who he felt like hearing from or favoring that day. The person that the hand belonged to got to share their thoughts on the material. It was typical to see certain humble men appointed to the role of ministerial servant and later elder become arrogant and self-righteous with that kind of unilateral power over others. If anyone complained or brought it up, the hurtful actions of the elders were explained away as the victim of the harassment needing to be humble, the victim often being called rebellious.

Then there was the ministry. Mostly, it was door-to-door, sometimes at someone's home writing letters, but there was always unsolicited advice sprinkled with gossip. Criticism, sometimes to an abusive level, was masked as concern or as though it was out of Christian love.

Here are a few examples: Always physically active, I had started to dabble in the newest trend of the moment, Pilates and yoga. One day, in the door-to-door ministry, I made the mistake of sharing this in one of the car groups I was in. The next time one of the women from that car group saw me at the meeting, she had researched the subject in the organization's archives and handed me one of the organization's magazines turned to the page about yoga explaining that it was pagan. She stated if I continued to practice yoga, she would feel compelled to mark me, choosing not to associate with me even though I wasn't disfellowshipped. How I exercised was cause for scrutiny.

Another time I was out in the door-to-door ministry in a car group of older women, and the subject of dress and grooming was brought up. As I engaged in their discussion and asked questions, I realized I was the focus of their disgust. My dresses were too tight, too short, and too low cut. They felt the poor brothers in the congregation were being tempted every time I came to a meeting dressed so inappropriately. How I looked was a problem.

Enrolled in the ministry school, I had my very first talk in my new congregation. It is basically a five-minute skit that you write and deliver in front of the congregation with another female if you are a woman and solo if you are a man. Apparently, women need a householder to preach to, but men command an audience. You are assigned a subject and an area to work on from their Ministry School Guidebook and critiqued publicly (currently, it is now private) from the stage by the overseer after you present. I was nervous, but I had worked hard and practiced a lot, so I felt ready.

After I presented, I took my seat and anxiously awaited my counsel. What came at me was nothing less than a barrage of criticism and angry chastisement. The overseer had misread my assignment number; he mistook a zero for an eight and thought I had the gull to write a talk working on my own topic and not his.

"Did you even read directions from the chapter I assigned you in the guidebook?" all while I tried to signal to him that the assignment written on my slip from him was what I had read up on, written, practiced, and presented. Humiliated, I left the meeting in tears. Later, I was told he felt he needed to come down on me hard because the congregation needed to know you can't do your own thing in meetings, especially when it came to the Ministry School. Even when he was shown the slip and the evidence revealed it was his mistake, he never apologized. I received no further assignments until a new overseer took the school over many months later.

Eventually, I made the decision to transfer back into my parents' congregation. It was allowed because I worked in Eureka, so it made sense to help me attend more meetings as I could just go to meetings there on my way home from work. Part of the procedure with such a transfer is to send an introductory letter to the new congregation along with the publisher's file, a compilation of any and everything you have been involved in, notes and details. All this is very confidential, not even the individual whose information is contained in the file is allowed to ever read what's in it.

One day at my parents' home, I went into my dad's desk to retrieve a pen. In the desk drawer, I saw a letter tucked away with my name on it. I did the unthinkable... I opened it and read it. It was my introductory letter to my parents' congregation. In the letter, an elder from the congregation I had left spoke of me kindly at first but then made the statement "Julia has said that her husband is off on Sundays, and she has made a promise to him to spend Sundays with him and not come to meetings." It went on to suggest that this is a dangerous compromise and the reason I wasn't making spiritual progress. I had confided in one elder and his wife the conflict I felt to have only every other Sunday off, and that because that was the only day to spend with my mate, it was hard to come to meetings. I had said it was hard, but I had never said I wasn't going to come to meetings on Sunday. Shouldn't my mate come first anyway? My words had been twisted, the misinformation documented in this letter, and I would now be judged by all the elders who would ever read this secret letter. Not to mention the very fact that I could never correct the information as I was barred from even knowing about the contents of the letter in the first place.

There is rarely truth in secrecy.

Then there were the get-togethers, if I was even invited because I had an unbelieving mate. We held a surprise anniversary party for my parents. Parties were acceptable if you appointed an elder to be the director of the feast. That man was put in charge of making sure that nothing got out of control or looked worldly at your get-together. He controlled the whole party. In addition to planning the guest list, the theme, the food, and how to get my parents to the venue, the music we would play was also heavily scrutinized. We had to remove several songs because they had adultery implied or stated or the artist was rumored to dabble in the occult or live a debauched lifestyle. We got all those details squared away, and the day of the party finally arrived. It was all so exciting, especially when we pulled it all off. My parents were surprised, and the evening was fun. We were in the middle of the party when I was approached by one of the elders as I danced with my then husband. He told me I was dancing seductively and needed to tone it down because there were children and single people present. I was not grinding or dirty dancing. My hands were above my head, raising my skirt a couple of inches shorter, and that was, in his opinion, inappropriate. I was dancing with my own husband! My husband, at the time, uncomfortable with the whole evening and all the religion talk, left the party after that.

Both my marriage and my religion were full of demands that could never be fully met. But then, I added a third party, the company I worked for.

The Employer

As the manager of the store, the hourly work requirements were high: forty-eight hours a week, six days every other week, open to close at least every Friday (twelve-and-a-half-hour day). If there were special events or peak seasons (Christmas, Mother's Day, Valentine's Day, etc.), these also required extra hours of work. From Thanksgiving to Christmas, there were two mandated days off and open to close most of the rest of the days. Some weeks during this period would consist of seventy-plus hour stretches with no days off.

But that was just the beginning.

Reports were generated daily, letting you know how you were doing, the "standards." Obtaining all five of the standards was required. Where once attaining daily sales was the requirement to be considered a performer, now driving all lines of business was the minimum. My team and my store did well, but it came at a price. There were high highs and very low lows. On the highs, I won trips to exciting places that I never would've gone to on my own. I won awards at the annual meetings, which were held inside Disney World in Florida, giving the sensation of being successful and accepted for just a moment before being sent home to drive business that exceeded last year again and again and again...and again.

But then, there were the lows, times when the economy was not healthy, or my team was in a rebuilding phase, and the numbers weren't where corporate felt they should be. This is when the pressure would come down on me hard. I was told then that there were no excuses, and I needed to find a way to do business. If we were up, I would be exhausted from the push. If we were down, I blamed myself and didn't leave the store for fear that I would be questioned as to why I would leave my team when the day/month/year was down. I remember feeling so exhausted, stretched, and anxious much of the time. To say I wasn't inspirational, encouraging, or fun for anyone to be around in those moments would be an understatement. I tried to do it all and be available to everyone, but some days, I wasn't anything but negative, angry, and moody. I saw the looks exchanged when I lost my cool.

Up or down, I was exhausted.

I felt the distance from everyone in all the areas of my life when I was empty and needed help. It seemed no one appreciated, wanted to support, or even liked being around me then. In hindsight, I don't think I even liked me during those times.

Sometimes I would cry out to God, angry that I was left alone, and He was nowhere to be found. Not one to wait for Him, maybe not ever truly believing in Him, I would pick myself up, saying, "Never mind, I can do this." Always easier to do things myself than look to a god that might punish me for asking for anything anyway.

I was pulled in three directions all day, every day. The religion I was a part of taught me that spirituality came from following their guidelines and not deviating. I believed I couldn't ask God for anything personal, including strength or guidance.

The lie was believing that I personally could please all people in all areas of my life, and if I didn't, there must be something wrong and defective in me. In the process, there were moments when I felt I was doing everything I could, but none of the people in my life were ever satisfied. I would wonder when I was maxed out why I couldn't keep up the pace. My life felt like I was a hamster on a wheel that had to go on and on until I died. I believed this was the life God had for me, and if I was tired, I must be doing something sinful or wrong.

The truth is, when God asks you to do anything, He provides the means and the way to do it. It won't come at any cost to you physically, mentally, emotionally, or spiritually that He doesn't supply in surplus. But daily, you must give your burdens to Him. He directs and completes it all, not me.

> "I can do all this through him who gives me strength." (Philippians 4:13 NIV)

> "But those who trust in the Lord will find new strength. They will soar high on wings like eagles. They will run and not grow weary. They will walk and not faint." (Isaiah 40:31 NLT)

I was on the hamster wheel for seventeen years until one day I looked away from the wire in front of me, tripped, and fell off.

CHAPTER 13

I've Fallen and I Can't Get Up

I had been going along for many years, trying to please and fill others' needs at all costs when my health began to show signs of weakening. My mind and body were warring, and my body was losing.

As far back as I can remember, my stress has always manifested itself in my gut. Constipation, painful stomachaches, and bloating were the earliest memories. As I progressed in my career, so did my symptoms. At first, the diagnosis was irritable bowel syndrome, a generic diagnosis given to a lot of patients at that time when there was no other clear diagnosis. My physician turned me onto magnesium therapy. With high doses of magnesium alleviating the symptoms, I could control my discomfort and carry on with my lifestyle of people-pleasing.

Then within my first year of managing, I was having trouble sleeping as I was riddled with anxiety. I worried about everything from what my husband's needs were and if I was taking care of him properly, to getting to all the congregation meetings, fulfilling my duties in the church and family, and of course, whether my store was up or down, if I was staffed and on and on and on.

I called the number on the poster at work for counseling, the Employee Assistance Program. I was given five sessions of complimentary therapy to help me deal with my anxiety. My therapist listened intently for a session or two, asked a few strategic questions, and took extensive notes. Midway through my third session, she suggested I think about making some lifestyle changes to reduce stress. One of the stresses in my life was trying to make it to those sessions at 8:00 a.m. before my ten- to twelve-hour shifts. So I decided to quit therapy.

My husband at the time grew tired of hearing me complain, and to make me stop, he would shout, "Just quit then!" But I knew he would not be okay with me earning a small salary with none of the perks of trips and bonuses. I constantly feared what would happen if he was not okay.

Two years into my position as store manager, the implosion began, quite literally. I was bleeding excessively with my monthly menstrual cycles and had to be treated for endometriosis. Monthly injections that put me in menopause for six months, I was told, would alleviate the symptoms for a few years. But that brought on an entirely other set of issues with extreme mood swings, hot flashes, and insomnia. Within a year after the last injection, the original issues were back with a vengeance. Now, however, the bleeding was out of control and not manageable. It was suggested that my lifestyle of constant stress was taking a toll on my body.

After five years of managing, I decided the answer was to quit my job. I collected my last annual bonus, paid off any bills we had, banked the rest, and quit. I had no job lined up and no idea of what I wanted to do next. I was convinced that I could work at a different job and not get consumed by it. Then I would have more time for my then husband and for the church.

Within a week, I was being criticized by all parties.

My parents and friends at church told me that quitting my job was unreasonable and unbalanced.

My husband had said he was onboard with my decision but quickly changed his mind when he felt added pressure of being the only one with income in the house. When I told my parents about his change of heart, they chastised me for quitting my job and suggested I was showing a lack of submission to my mate, which could result in losing God's favor. The validation I thought I would finally get from that organization, or my parents, was nowhere to be found.

The team I had put together to run the store before I left the company, my succession plan, struggled. Most resigned within a few weeks. For some reason, I took responsibility for that as well. I felt as if I had somehow failed as a manager because they didn't stay together when I left. Unreasonable, to say the least.

The first week, my husband humored me as I researched what I may want to do next and said he wanted to do the same thing as soon as I was established in my new career. Although I had quit the demanding job, I hadn't changed my mind set or addressed any of the lies that kept me running. Instead, I made a tight schedule, cramming in everything I could think of to make everyone happy and, in effect, make myself valuable to those I loved. Every day on my calendar was planned out. I had days of the week for everything—door-to-door, cleaning the house, searching for a new career, and of course, a weekly shared day off with my husband. I made myself even busier than before.

During this time, a longtime friend (not part of the religion) suggested I come to Santa Rosa to visit her with some of my now free time. Once down there, she tried her best to help me loosen up a little. The first night we made cocktails and hot-tubbed, reminiscing and laughing a lot. The next day, she suggested we take an impromptu trip to San Francisco, rent a room downtown, and be tourists. I was so scared; for what reason, I can't explain. The entire time we were there, going through China Town, riding the trolley, visiting historic venues, I couldn't relax. She was so sweet and encouraging and never berated me once for being so uptight. The last night of our mini getaway we went to a cute little bistro for dinner where she tried to open a conversation about my religion, suggesting the possibility that it could be contributing to my stress. She expressed her concern over my mental and emotional state and gently asked if religion was part of the problem. Defensive, my walls came up quickly, and that was the end of the fun getaway. She never brought it up again.

Instead of feeling refreshed and relaxed, I went home feeling guilty for having spent the time and money.

When I still didn't have an income within a few weeks, my then husband began to threaten that I better get a job soon come hell or high water—whatever that meant. Plus, he hated me home so much. One night, he came home to find another meal prepared and waiting for him. Feeling encroached upon, he flashed, "This is what I was afraid of! You cook dinner, and then I'm under pressure to come home and eat it!" My coddling was not appreciated or wanted at home. It was time to get a job, or two.

I took a part-time position in the office at the shopping mall and pursued a career in massage. The first Christmas outside of retail was odd for me. Although I had longed to have my evenings and weekends free, I felt uncomfortable and unsettled now that I did. My dream was to be free of the chains of jewelry sales, but now, I found myself longing to be back there.

I switched jobs and began working full time for friends of the family, members of the church, who owned a flooring store. I kept my massage business on the side as I really loved my clients and helping them unwind and heal.

Money was not the issue. Validation or lack of it hung over me, changing jobs hadn't fixed the personal inequity I saw in myself.

I received phone calls for the next three years, asking me to come back to the jewelry industry. If I'm being honest, I loved being pursued like that. I was enjoying my little massage business that I had built, making good money and being appreciated. But I had never done the work to fix the broken woman inside of me, nor had I realized God's love and acceptance of me, so the calm routine was not comfortable. Plus, my husband wanted to quit his job to find his happiness and couldn't do so on my massage and flooring job income. I was restless, unfulfilled, chasing whims, still blind to the higher power waiting for me to look up for my sense of belonging, contentment, and strength.

So within three years, I went back to the jewelry store as a manager and got right back on the hamster wheel, running with renewed vigor and determination. I was so grateful to be making big paychecks, not to mention receiving positive feedback again. I was able to financially contribute to excess once again.

The company my then husband was employed with was downsizing, and with my income booming, he was able to take the buyout and go back to school for job retraining. He was ecstatic; life was good.

The next few years were like groundhog day. Every day I was juggling home, religion/family, and work. All three had their own demands. Every night ending with me exhausted, stressed, and hopeless. My religion taught me not to ask God for anything secular. He's there for you to strive after, not for Him to give to you. Unless you are asking Him for the strength to do the things required within the religion to serve the congregation or elders, which is equal to serving God himself.

My husband had taken a position with the postal service, but it was a temporary position that gave him no Union protection and, therefore, no defined days off, paid holidays, or any other benefits. He is someone who likes routine, so again, he was unhappy, and so again, I felt the pressure to remedy that. I bought him any and every toy and trinket he could want. He would adore me for a few weeks until the shiny wore off, and he coveted something else or secluded deeper into himself, the quiet, convincing me he was drifting away from me. When that happened, I always equated it to me not being enough for him. In hindsight? He had his own personal internal struggles. He, too, was looking for things to complete him, filling a hole from a wound that was there long before me. It wasn't my place to even attempt to fill it, but I continued to try.

The excitement of Julia coming back to the store began to fade within six months, and with it, the pressure began to mount again for me to perform bigger and better than the year before. My very capable assistant manager (who was the same religion) got promoted and moved away, doubling my workload and removing my source of spiritual encouragement on a workday. I had always been trained to have a bench of employees, all ready to move up, so I quickly promoted a very aggressive performer to the vacated position.

I thought all was well until I received a phone call one evening while I was relaxing at home a few days after one of our peak seasons. One of my full-timers was leaving with no notice. She stated that the assistant, now pregnant, was prone to aggressive outbursts up to and including kicking things when she was enraged. The associate told me she was leaving whether I did something or not but encouraged me to intervene for the rest of the staff. I called Human Resources for back up, and they gave no guidelines or support. Did I witness it? No. Did any other associate corroborate the story? No one came forward; no one collaborated on the stories. Human Resources strongly advised nothing could be done; leave it alone!

My assistant had her baby a few months later and quickly came back to work as she was the sole financial provider in her home. I did a lot of training in her absence and now have two very capable full-time employees completing the team. We all welcomed her back with open arms, ready to start producing the numbers together. Within a month, one of my key holders reported some very unprofessional and disturbing behavior. I took it to my district manager, a sales driving businessman with no interest in details, who told me to stop getting involved in gossip and focus on business. I took my concerns to the inner circle of support at the church to ask for advice. They felt I should try to get rid of her because her behavior was sin-filled.

In hindsight, if I really had been in tune with the Lord and what He wants from me, the love and grace and mercy that He's shown to each of us, I would've seen her through that lens. She clearly was in crisis, maybe even battling postpartum. Instead of reacting with loving-kindness, I self-righteously turned my back on her, making her feel even worse. She needed a mentor and guidance, a shoulder to lean on; she was lost. Instead, I gave her judgment and the cold shoulder, wanting her to know I was disappointed that she wasn't fulfilling the role I had given her.

Fear and trepidation filled the store.

Anxiety and stress were my daily companions.

Between my stomach and uterus, I was in constant pain, borderline hemorrhaging most of the month even. I was sent in for an emergency colonoscopy, the word *cancer* being thrown around as something we needed to rule out. In recovery, I was told I was fine; the internal hemorrhoids, the doctor believed, were from working out too hard, and I was sent home.

But the bleeding became so excessive my doctor asked me to come in to discuss hysterectomy as an option. I scheduled the appointment on my own, no idea that my then husband should or would want to be a part of the decision.

The day of the consultation, I was shocked when the exam room door opened and in walked my then husband. He wanted to be there for the consultation. The doctor laid out all the options. He paused and asked, "Are you certain you want to do this? You don't have any children." I looked at my husband for the answer. I got a blank stare. I knew how he felt about having children, but this was permanent. He said nothing. I told the doctor we were sure, and we planned the surgery for eight weeks later.

In hindsight, I understand now that he had always been so adamant about not having children, not because he didn't want to have a child with me, which is what I believed all those years, but because he was afraid to be a parent. In that moment in the exam room, he was just as unsure about the permanent decision we were about to make, but he was equally afraid to voice that.

In the meantime, I had been selected to be a delegate for my religious organization at an international convention in Berlin, Germany. I was so excited. I remember feeling like I had done it; I had finally been deemed acceptable to God, and this was a sign of that acceptance.

The flight was long but filled with anticipation. I had never flown internationally. I made some friends, other single women, and after the first full day, we all decided to have a meal together. We went around the table telling each other a little bit about ourselves. After I finished, one of them, my assigned roommate, nonetheless, said with total disgust dripping from her mouth, "Well, I can't believe your congregation let someone with an unbelieving mate represent them at this convention."

I recoiled, shocked to have their kind acceptance retracted so quickly from me. When I tried to defend my marital status to the group, even telling them that my congregation was supportive, we had quite a few women with unbelieving mates, this seemed to anger her even more. She stated, "Well, if that was my congregation, I would transfer out. Clearly, there is an unclean spirit there." That was the end of dinner. I spent the rest of my trip either alone or with another young woman and her mom. I sat by myself at the convention, with no interaction from other delegates. There were several thousand in attendance; it was held at Olympia Park Berlin, at capacity (approximately seventy thousand). I came home exhausted and disillusioned.

A few weeks later, I went out on a six-week leave for my hysterectomy. My husband at the time took a leave of absence to take care of me. After the surgery, I was hospitalized for two nights. I was diagnosed with endometriosis, a fibroid tumor, and pelvic congestion disorder. My body was literally imploding from stress and lifestyle choices.

The first morning, my dad came to see me. I sat up like the little trooper I always tried to be for him, smiling at my guest to make him feel comfortable. My husband arrived with some coffee for me, and all three of us sipped coffee until, overcome with nausea, I spontaneously vomited out all my coffee. My dad's face turned white, and he left shortly after that. During the rest of my hospital stay, he never came back. I had a few visitors. When they left, I felt alone, and darkness would begin to press down on me. I tried to read religious literature or play the CDs of Kingdom Melodies (music with no lyrics used at congregation meetings), but the morphine drip I was on made it difficult to concentrate.

I didn't find God in any of those things, which made me feel forsaken and abandoned.

On the last day, my husband came in just as they were discharging me and took me home. At first, he was quite attentive. He helped me up to the bathroom and brought me food, water, and my ibuprofen as needed. But a few days into my healing I would wake up to the sound of war in the living room, the Call of Duty video game. Within the week, he was fully sucked into a life of gaming. I didn't recognize then, but now I understand he was self-medicating his broken heart, his loss. At the time, I felt like he was annoyed with me, that he didn't really want the burden of my care. Never once did I think about what he had just lost; he had always said he didn't want children, but now, we couldn't have them together either. We should've been comforting each other, but instead, he buried himself in gaming; and I sat in my bed at night, watching movies and crying.

One night, I called my sister, and when she said hello, I was crying so hard I couldn't speak. I told her I was lonely; no one was coming to see me, and in the quiet, there was so much heartache that I could not explain. She was having a health crisis of her own (she didn't know at the time, but her clavicle artery had collapsed). I remember her being so angry that no one was there for me. She got off the phone and called my parents. She called back to tell me they would try to come see me, but Dad was giving a talk out of town that weekend so it would be after that. She called an elder in my congregation, and he told me he wasn't the overseer assigned to me but would investigate it. He was a kind man and called me back, sympathized, and then said, "I will call your overseer, and he will reach out to you." I never heard from any of the leaders in my congregation again. More on that later.

I started drinking bottles of wine in the evening, the good expensive ones from my collection. I will never forget the one night I decided (stupidly) to watch the movie *Seven Pounds* while drinking wine. Halfway through the movie, the reality of my uterus being gone sunk in. I would never conceive of a child with my husband. I would never give birth. I called my best friend at the time, distraught as I told her I just realized I'm never going to be a mom.

She snapped, "I knew you weren't okay! I asked you last week if you were okay, and you said you were fine. You lied to me!" That was the last time I cried about my uterus, the last time I asked anyone for comfort. Instead, I turned my attention to healing my physical body, finding the perfect piece of jewelry to commemorate my loss, and getting myself back to work. During the last two weeks of my leave, my then husband put down the gaming control during the day and took up painting the exterior of the house. Our routine became a walk around the block in the morning (approximately one mile), me lying on the grass resting while he painted, another walk at night, and ending with me in bed and him gaming until one in the morning.

As I began to heal, I also returned to the congregation meetings, excited for some encouragement and determined to feel God's approval. Once I arrived, the friends didn't even look away from whoever they were chatting with; many didn't even greet me. I slipped out after the meetings unnoticed. A few would call to check on me but met my state of hurt and loneliness with the assumption that my faith and trust were damaged from the weeks of no meeting attendance. I had a meeting with my overseer one night after the meeting and tried to describe what the past few weeks had been like. "I'm sorry your faith is damaged, but I don't know what that has to do with me" were his words. That was the last time I asked that man to shepherd me as one of God's sheep.

The last weekend of our leave together, we went away for the weekend, as sort of a last hoorah before we both returned to work. We were in Costco looking for a new TV for the bedroom, and I roamed over to the jewelry case. He met me over there several minutes later, new TV in the cart, and asked what I was doing. I told him I still hadn't found my uterus necklace, and I thought I would look at one in the case.

He blurted out, "When is this going to be over already?! This has been going on for six weeks!"

I was speechless, stunned. The dream of being a mother someday, part of my feminine identity, was gone; and he expected me to get over it faster than my physical body could. I don't know what happened inside of me. I just felt something snap shut, the flow of love for him began to shut down. I believe this was when I began to resent him, all that our marriage was and all that I had relentlessly done to try to make it perfect. I remember feeling gravely misunderstood and unloved. We drove the four-hour drive home in silence.

Again, I had no spiritual background that would suggest I had a greater heavenly Father holding me tight in those moments, keeping me safe. I had no spiritual foundation for taking the pain to the Father and laying it at His feet, that He could heal me, my body, and my marriage.

I returned to work and tried to carry on business as usual, but nothing felt usual or normal anymore. I won another trip, and on the trip, I decided my unhappiness was my job, and I didn't want to work there anymore. Again, I thought the hole in my soul was from something on the exterior. I refused to look inside. I wasn't even aware I could look up.

I came home and began putting out the word in the community that I was looking for a new job. The family that owned the flooring store called me. I went in for a meeting one evening, they made me a generous offer to come back to work for them, and I accepted.

This should be where the happy ending begins. I relax, enjoy my time, and have enough income to generously contribute to my household and live content. But that is not what happened next.

The lie I believed was that God was not approachable for the everyday struggles of life. I believed it was wrong to ask for personal things. I knew money was essential for life on this earth, but I didn't trust Him to provide it. I had been hurt by his organization and didn't trust anyone, including my then husband or God himself, with my heart.

The truth is that God is the only one you can truly rely on, and He will never leave you or let you down. In my moments of weakness and seeming abandonment, I now know He was there waiting for me to reach out to Him and believe that He had everything I needed already taken care of. He is our provider and protector of all things big and small, and we can truly trust Him to be there for us day and night.

> "Keep your life free from love of money, and be content with what you have, for he has said, "I will never leave you nor forsake you." (Hebrews 13:5 ESV)

> "You haven't done this before. Ask using my name, and you will receive, and you will have abundant joy." (John 16:24 NLT)

> "Trust in the Lord with all your heart and lean not on you own understanding; in

all your ways submit to him, and he will make your paths straight." (Proverbs 3:5, 6 NIV)

So here I was, barren, halfway done with my life and yet still had not found any value or purpose in my existence.

The circumstances and decisions I made produced nothing short of a perfect storm that left me shipwrecked.

CHAPTER 14

The Winds of Change

Merriam-Webster defines the winds of change this way: "forces that have the power to change things, used generally to mean change is going to happen."

At this point, I should've been happy and content. Having children was no longer an option and, therefore, no longer an area of contention for my marriage. I'm able to go to all the meetings and have a full share in the ministry, so theoretically, I'm completely accepted by the religious organization I belong to.

We had plenty of money to save and spend. So my husband was content.

What happened next should've destroyed me. My choices were poor and inexcusable. I felt abandoned by my church, my friends, my family, and eventually even myself. At the same time, it's also why I know how very much I am loved even when I thought I was completely lost.

My brother-in-law called me up one day and told me my niece needed me. She had a new boyfriend and didn't want to be part of the religion anymore, and he knew I could talk some sense into her—his words, not mine. She and I met and had lunch. I wanted to be all tough love and tell her, "You shouldn't leave the organization," but my words had no bite. I said all the things I was supposed to, even used my life as an example of what not to do, but I didn't believe the words coming out of my own mouth, so how could she?

Within a few months, the big announcement came that she was pregnant, and they wanted to get married. It was bittersweet, of course. She was so young, barely a legal adult, but she was always so poised and mature, we all believed (wanted to believe) she had it all figured out. We were excited for her and supported her without questioning. The wedding was small: At my home, in the backyard, and my dad, her grampa, performed the ceremony. It was so beautiful. They became a newlywed couple, and my husband at the time accepted them as family. He hadn't accepted any of my family before that.

Life was good.

A few months went by, and we began preparing for her baby shower. Anticipation filled the air.

But there was something looming none of us saw coming.

Unbeknownst to us, our dad had been heavily scrutinized for performing the ceremony. When the other elders brought it to his attention, he didn't see anything wrong with it, and that is where the trouble really began. Whether it was one or more elders in his congregation, it is unclear, but an investigation ensued that even involved the traveling overseer. My dad was silent. This was his natural posture when it came to his family and his position in the congregation. He never had chosen us over them.

A circuit assembly was taking place on a Saturday a few weeks later; the shower was planned for the next day. It was to be a family shower, co-ed. At the assembly, as everyone was cleaning up the assembly hall and stacking chairs, my sisters and I stood in horror as we watched one of the elders in my dad's congregation visibly chastising our dad at the front of the auditorium for all to see using exaggerated movements of his arms to express his exasperation. We knew something bad was being said but had no idea the ugliness that was unfolding in front of us. My dad passed us on his way out and muttered that he would not be attending the baby shower. Mom later called and told us that if he did, the elder body had decided, he would be removed as an elder for his rebelliousness. I was absolutely disgusted, almost nauseous. The very same elder that self-righteously chastised my dad had performed the same ceremony for his own "worldly and immoral" grandson (his words now, not mine), I had been at the ceremony myself, just a few years before, in front of a crowd of hundreds! The hypocrisy didn't escape me.

Later that evening, I called a mature woman in the congregation, a dear friend of mine to vent. Her husband, another elder in an entirely different congregation, had already communicated to her the line that was being drawn in the proverbial sand. She told me that she couldn't go to the shower either. The baby shower was being boycotted by the religion as inappropriate. My niece had a husband and budding family and was happy. This wasn't acceptable to these men. They felt she should hold her head down in shame. This shower, in their opinion, was flaunting her sin with blatant disregard.

The next morning, I went to the gym before going to set up for the baby shower. I was on the elliptical with my MP3 player when the Black-Eyed Peas' "Where Is the Love" came on. I broke down in tears. I saw my religion for the first time and realized there is no love there. How could this be God's religion with this amount of judgmental unkindness. I was so disappointed in the god of this organization.

We didn't want to stumble our niece, her husband, and his family or my "unbelieving mate"; so we decided to keep the entire drama that had unfolded a secret from them. The shower was full of love, laughter, and fun and was well attended, with a few in the church and a lot of loyal worldly friends. Again, the irony.

A few weeks before her first grandbaby was born, my older sister, my niece's mother, discovered documentation that suggested her husband, living out of town at the time, was not being faithful. She took the information, which clearly showed an inappropriate relationship between her husband and a very young colleague of his, to the body of elders to get permission for a divorce. They refused to give weight to her or the evidence she submitted to them, suggesting, instead, that she just be patient and loyal to God and her husband, and it would all work out. If she chose to leave him, she would lose their support and, according to their teachings, God's approval.

Another chunk of our faith chiseled away. How could this be God's true religion, and if it is, how could God let us be hurt by His organization and not protect us?

The baby was born in April. One of the most joyous occasions of my life. She was beautiful and perfect and immediately, just like her mama, a part of my heart. I could not stop talking about her or sharing pictures of her to everyone that would listen and look.

My husband at the time was also enamored by her as well. "The kids," as we called the little family, began coming over for dinner weekly. I decided on my days off I was going to watch the baby. I arranged my work schedule to be there for the kids and the baby. I was excited to have time with them and to be able to help them out as well. My parents chastised me for being imbalanced. I was working full time; why would I take on this too? Friends from the church would question me; how could I sacrifice my time in the ministry for time with this baby?

Opinions from all circles were mixed, but all pointed to the fact that the birth of this beautiful child was touching and changing my heart and my life forever.

As I grew closer to the baby, all the years of stifling the pain of my own decisions, and quite frankly, the natural consequences of them, couldn't be contained any longer. Slowly, I began to crack open with emotions I didn't know how to express and thoughts I didn't know what to do with.

I had kept my massage business that consisted of a select handful of dependable clients. One of them was an older man, well known in the community. There was an unexplainable attraction there, one that should've led me to stop treating him immediately. But I didn't. One of the biggest mistakes I have ever made with a devastating set of consequences.

I started running longer and longer distances. On these runs, I would purge so much anger as I sorted through a variety of suppressed emotions. Running became my safe haven. It was the only place I felt any control in my life as I pushed my body to its limits.

I nagged my then husband to plan and take a vacation together, as I could see the wedge between us becoming unmanageable. The chasm grew bigger and bigger every weekend that he zoned out with video games or planned motorcycle riding getaways with his friends, which I wasn't invited to.

Again, in hindsight, I believe my now ex-husband was trying to deal with his own feelings about our decision not to have children together. Saying he didn't want a family for all those years was one thing, but now, that door was permanently closed to us. I couldn't see his journey through the lens of my own pain.

To be fair, I was not the best companion at this point. I was bitter and angry and trying to hide it but spilling it out on everyone. I still believed, though now begrudgingly so, that I was supposed to be silent and "win my husband without a word" (1 Peter 3:1, the religion's version).

I was angry my needs weren't being met but was equally afraid of abandonment from all sides if I stated those needs to anyone or acted needy.

This battle within me went on for several months.

One weekend, my sister and I kept the baby so the parents could go away for their first wedding anniversary. The weekend was the same weekend as the fall circuit assembly. We proudly brought the baby together. We held her and fed her and tried to share our precious baby with the masses. But we were met with judging glances and whispers. My dad kept his distance physically, angry at this point that his children had caused him more embarrassment and problems; and my mom, medicated, walked around, completely dazed and unemotional. One man even acted like the baby was contaminated, recoiling when we almost bumped into him. During the closing song of that day's session, I couldn't even sing. I stood holding that beautiful baby in my arms and cried silently. I knew something irreversible to my faith in that organization and subsequently in God had transpired that day. On the drive home, I divulged it all to my very hurt sister, the baby's gramma. She suggested I seek therapy. She pleaded with me to go get the help I needed and deserved before walking away from the church. She still held hope that God was in that organization.

I was emotionally abandoned by my parents, my husband, and the religion I thought was the key to God's approval and acceptance.

What happened next is neither acceptable nor excusable, but one could say it was foreseeable.

Instead of distancing myself from the client I spoke of earlier, I continued to see him (more regularly actually) and began confiding in him. He also suggested I find a good therapist, seemingly so supportive at a time that I had no support.

I told my then husband I needed to get therapy for my past and the unhealed wounds that I carried with me. He shook his head in disbelief and told me, "Do what you need to do." His way of dealing with any unwanted negative emotions was to ignore them until they dulled, and he desperately needed me to do the same.

The day of my first appointment, I was nervous. My then husband and I had our morning coffee together and made a plan for the day. I would go to my appointment, go get the baby, have her for the day, and after the kids picked her up, he and I would talk about what came out of my appointment. All went according to plan until the kids came to pick up the baby, and he invited them to go eat with us. He didn't want to talk about my therapy session, that was between me and my therapist, and he didn't want to get involved with it. I was so disappointed, and I'm sure I didn't hide it very well.

The next week in therapy, I opened to my therapist a little more. I talked about all this unexplained anger and bitterness I had toward everyone in my life and how ashamed I was to be acting this way. She listened intently and gently asked me if it really was unexplained. She asked a few questions, and the answers opened wounds I hadn't looked at in years. Together, we talked about all the sacrifices I had made, pushing myself to take care of everyone and not taking care of myself. She gave me a small notepad and suggested I start writing down my thoughts and feelings so as to find resolutions and solutions, small basic changes that I could make in my reactions and behavior. For the first time, as I journaled, I realized I didn't know what was true about anything—myself, my life, or God. I remember driving away, feeling like an egg with a huge crack and not knowing what was about to hatch from it.

That afternoon, when my then husband got off work and the baby was napping, emboldened by the validation I had received at the therapist's office, I told my husband how I felt I made a lot of sacrifices, and now I found myself wondering what's in it for me in all areas of my life. He was irritated.

He didn't want to talk about any of this and proclaimed, "You know what? You aren't the only one who made sacrifices. I made some pretty big ones too."

I calmly asked him what sacrifices he felt he made that I wasn't seeing, and he blurted out, "I didn't want to marry you! I had been married and never wanted to do that again, but I sacrificed and married you!"

Stunned, I got up and left the room to check on the baby. Maybe I should've sat and asked more questions; maybe I should've told him how much that hurt. But I didn't. I never tried to talk to him about my progress again. I recoiled emotionally even more and never trusted him again.

This was the beginning of the end of our marriage.

I saw the male client the next night, and he asked how things were going. I confided I enjoyed the therapy but had no one to share it with. He suggested that after my next appointment, we meet for coffee; he would love to hear about it. I knew better; everything inside of me screamed "No!" My intuition knew it was not a good idea to intimately confide one on one to another man, especially since my marriage was struggling.

I didn't listen.

My new routine was going to therapy, meeting up with the man with a sympathetic ear, going to pick up the baby, and holding her tightly all day. Before long, the lines of appropriate behavior began to blur. The more I received therapy and the sympathetic ear and shoulder from the other man, the more I began to despise my marriage, my parents, my religious organization, and in effect, God.

The disassembling of my life and plummeting into the other man's arms went quickly. Within weeks of our first inappropriate text, we were fully involved.

During therapy, the incident from the jetty in which I almost drowned came up. I shared the memory and the subsequent nightmares I was having of the waves trying to take me under as I desperately grabbed at blades of grass as they broke off in my hands and how I would wake up scared even though it was a dream. My therapist suggested I reach out to my parents to discuss the incident and get more insight. Because of his lack of loyalty to his family and his cowering to the elders for his validation, at this point in time, I didn't really have much of a relationship with my dad. My mom had been taking a lot of prescriptions and, therefore, was not very coherent and our mother/daughter bond had suffered. I decided to email the journey I was on to my parents, addressing them both in the email. Their collective responses were those I mentioned in chapter 2. My response was to ask them to give me some space. I didn't want to hear any more excuses and justification for why I wasn't cared for by anyone that was supposed to care for me.

Thanksgiving and the weekend that followed were the straws that broke my proverbial back. My sister, now separated from her husband, came to dinner at my in-laws with me. This was a huge step for her as she had never celebrated Thanksgiving as a devout member of our church. She sat around the newly decorated Christmas tree with my mother-in-law and me, her face beaming with newfound excitement. After a few glasses of wine, I began to share with my mother-in-law, who was also one of my closest friends, my journey and how I was feeling so resentful and bitter. She seemed surprised and asked me to elaborate. I told her a few things I had been working on in therapy, up to and including giving up having children to be married to her son. Taken completely off guard at my revelation and probably unable to process it, she got up, brushed down her apron, and said, "Well, I don't know what to tell you about that," and left the room. Conversation over. She was adept at making things okay for everyone as well, and this road of self-exploration was not one she wanted either of us to continue on.

The next day, some friends of ours came to visit for the weekend. On the morning before they left, my friend and I were alone outside having our morning coffee. I confided to her that the lack of intimacy and communication in my marriage was making me unbearably unhappy, and I didn't know what to do. She stared at me blankly and said, "Well, just talk to him." I had just told her he didn't want anything to do with any conversation involving my healing and that was her response?

Another friend that didn't know what to say—another dead end for help.

The clencher came on that Sunday. I had not attended any meetings since the circuit assembly several weeks before. I went to the meeting desperate to hear from God. During the study, there was a paragraph in the magazine being studied that day that specifically stated that if you are struggling in any way, mentally/physically/emotionally, it must be your faith. You must be missing meetings, not studying, and not associating. The problem with your broken heart is, quite frankly, you. I hadn't been going to their meetings, studying, or associating; but it was because I had been broken by them, not the other way around!

That was it. I left the meeting hysterically crying, my faith in pieces. Upon my arrival home, my husband was just getting home from his errands as well and met me in the garage, shocked at my emotional state. I started trying to explain through my tears that I was falling apart, like I had no one to turn to; no one cared to help, including my very own parents.

As if all he heard was the last few words, he yelled, "I'm tired of all this, Julie! God! This doesn't involve me. It's between you and them. I'm done listening!" He turned, walked into the house, and the door slammed behind him. The tears stopped for a while that day, and a new feeling began to grow—hate. To this day, I cringe every time someone calls me Julie. That version of my name reminds me of the last time I poured out my heart to a man and trusted him to help me and the subsequent door slamming in my face as the answer.

I had built my faith on man, and man had failed me; therefore, God had failed me.

As I turned my back on my religion, I searched for someone to make me feel whole. The male client became my closest friend and, then quickly, my adulterous lover. It was wrong on so many levels, all of it, but my damaged heart convinced me I needed that other man, deserved him, and his kindness. I craved his words that embraced me with approval.

But the "heart is deceitful" (Jeremiah 17:9 NIV). The pain I brought into my life, my marriage, and so many close to me that were subsequently affected by that selfish move was nothing anyone ever deserves.

I had thoroughly deceived myself; the consequences were devastating to everyone near me. Chapter 1 gives you a small overview of the pain it caused, but the decision to engage in that affair hurt many, many people. The kind of pain that only God can heal.

The lie I had believed my entire life that came crashing down was that a man-made organization can and did represent God here on earth. I truly believed that the organization was delivering the unkind unloving and harshness straight from God's lips to their tyrannical ears, giving them the authority to hurt others without any consequence to themselves. When I stood up for myself, I believed I had to walk away from God to do so.

The truth is that God can use men in all their imperfections, but He prefers to talk to each of us directly and lovingly. We should never focus on what one group of men preaches and teaches as if it is the gospel of Jesus, especially when their words and behaviors contrast with His words. God is the god of love. Anything taught contrary to that is the biggest lie you can believe.

That was the biggest lie of my life.

> Do not put your trust in princes, in human beings, who cannot save. When their spirit departs, they return to the ground; on that very day their plans come to nothing. Blessed are those whose help is in the God of Jacob, whose hope is in the Lord their God. He is the Maker of heaven and earth, the sea, and everything in them—he remains faithful forever. (Psalm 146:3–6 NIV)

> "Dear friends, let us continue to love one another, for love comes from God. Anyone who loves is a child of God and knows God. But anyone who does not love does not know God, for God is love." (1 John 4:7, 8 NLT)

So there it is, how I got there on that beach. The whale breaching in that moment was a beautiful gift, a God wink, but it only scratched the surface of what God was willing to do to show me who He really is. He hadn't ever left me; He had pursued me.

Eventually, to get me alone, just Him and me, like a mama kitty, He had picked me up by the tuft of my neck and brought me somewhere safe to reveal to me all things I was told that I truly believed about Him, were lies.

He brought so many people into my life to love me in the days that followed. Friends and new family, including my now husband, Keith. I would go for long runs on that beautiful island in those days and ask God many questions looking for answers. Sometimes on those runs, a beautiful cardinal would fly next to me just as I was wondering if God was on this journey with me. The redheaded cardinal is my Jesus bird, a sign that whatever I was praying about in that moment, God was listening. Ask God for signs; He will generously give. Another of His many loving and personal gifts.

Keith is the one that took me to church for the first time in my life. I was so afraid I was committing the ultimate sin of apostasy that first time through the doors. But as I listened to the worship band sing and praise God, all I could do was cry. I couldn't deny His presence there, healing me. I knew He was guiding me; He was with me and had never left me.

I eventually joined a small women's group where we studied Beth Moore's *Secrets*. During one of those studies, as the other women went around the circle sharing their feelings about their personal relationship with Jesus, I sat quietly and cried because I didn't understand what that felt like. I longed to have that, to feel that. The women lovingly, without any judgment whatsoever, prayed over me. One of the women spoke such kindness about God wanting me to know He loves me and forgives me for all the mistakes I had been holding over myself, even the most shameful ones. That night on the drive home, I prayed in a deep, personal way to God. I asked Jesus if what was said was true; did He really forgive me? In that moment, as my left hand held the steering wheel and my right hand rested on the center console, I felt a warm, comforting sensation in my right hand. It was as if the Lord himself held my hand. I knew then, as I know now, He was there, always had been; and I am truly forgiven and always have been.

For years now, I have felt compelled to tell the world what a loving caregiver He really is.

To all that have been beaten with the Bible instead of being soothed by its words and those that have had their hearts ripped out in the name of religion, read this over and over until you believe the *truth*.

He *loves* you! God is not behind any of this!

Jesus came to this earth to save us, show us another way to live by his personal example, and have it closely documented for generations. He gave His life for that, for us.

That is love.

I wrote this book to tell a real love story. The truth about our Creator and His never-ending pursuit. He was always there for me even when I couldn't see it, and He does the same for you. We are His beloved.

When we feel lost, we just need to look up; He's there.

If someone is telling you He has left you because of anything you said or did or thought, they are misguided and misinformed.

If your inner voice screams you are unworthy of His love, no matter where that voice started or who spoke the lies over you first, you can silence it with the truth in His word.

He wants each of us to know the truth about Him. His love, and the depths He has gone to, goes to and will continue going to in His pursuit of you.

He is love, and because of that, we are perfectly loved.

We are never lost; we are always loved. The journey to discover that fact started on a beach but continues year after year. But that, my friends, is another beautiful discussion to be shared another day.

ABOUT THE AUTHOR

Julia was born and spent the first forty years of her life in Humboldt County, California. She then moved to Kaua'i, Hawai'i, where she met her husband, Keith. Together, they now reside with their daughter in Las Vegas, Nevada. Julia and her family attend The Crossing LV where she serves beside her husband on the prayer team.

Julia has worked for the same company in sales for thirty-three years; however, she has always had various other interests as well. She holds a certificate in wellness coaching from Cornell University, is a certified massage practitioner, and has had a lucrative massage business. She also earned certifications in fitness instruction where she spent a decade supplementing her income teaching fitness classes as well. Her entire career has been based on helping others find joy and feel good about themselves while supporting herself financially.

Although Julia has always believed in God, she broke away from a legalistic religion twelve years ago and now enjoys the freedom to truly read God's word, speak to God, and hear his voice directly. That intimate relationship with the One that created her has been both healing and empowering. Although she has no formal training in literacy studies, she felt called to write her story to help others with similar backgrounds feel good about who they are in Christ and what they were created to do.

Printed in the USA
CPSIA information can be obtained
at www.ICGtesting.com
CBHW030332011224
18019CB00009B/4